SOCCER'S SUPERSTARS

by
ROBERT GOLDSTEIN
and
GARY WOHL

A Tempo Star Book

Distributed by Ace Books
Grosset & Dunlap, Inc., Publishers
New York, N.Y. 10010
A Filmways Company

For Our Parents

ACKNOWLEDGMENTS

We would like to thank Jim Trecker, Director of Public Relations of the North American Soccer League, and Amy Oakley, his efficient and charming assistant. Also, to our editor, Mark Becker, for his patience.

CONTENTS

A selection of photographs follows page 147.

SOCCER'S SUPERSTARS

INTRODUCTION

When the New York Cosmos won their first NASL championship in 1972, some 6,000 people turned out to watch the game at Hofstra University on Long Island. Five years later, about the same number of fans cheered the Cosmos' second championship game victory. The only difference was that the 1977 crowd showed up *after* the title match—at New York's Kennedy International Airport to welcome the triumphant Cosmos home from Portland, Oregon.

If statistics measure the vital signs of individual athletes and teams, attendance figures have been the electrocardiogram blips of life for the whole sport of soccer in America. And the diagnosis is clear; there is no need for a second opinion. Soccer is alive and, well, kicking in the U.S. At the championship game in Portland, 35,548 people filled Civic Stadium. Earlier, for their two playoff games, the Cosmos drew more than 150,000 fans. The also-ran Minnesota Kicks attracted 32,771 per game.

But while figures may tell a story, people are the story. Without a doubt, it was one remarkable human being, Pele, who brought America out of its soccer coma. Wherever he played, the King of Soccer won new subjects—both for himself and the game. By the time he retired after three years in the U.S., soccer, the planetary pastime, had found a highly respectable niche in the one major country in the world that had long scorned it. As Pele said after his last game, "Now I know I have accomplished what I came here for—to make soccer a reality in the U.S."

That reality has been established not only by the NASL's turnstile counts, but also by a phenomenal rise in participation in soccer. From 1960 to 1977, the number of boys and girls in organized leagues jumped from 114,000 to close to a million. For sure, one reason why so many families attend NASL matches, is that youngsters are getting their folks to take them to see the pros play their new game.

And some of the best pros is what this book is about. At the same time that Pele was filling stadia in America, he helped to lure top players from Europe and South America to the NASL. Understandably, little is known in the U.S. about the stars who shone in their home countries and throughout the soccer world, about their triumphs, their skills, their personalities. But they seem here to stay.

You'll also meet some American superstars, the vanguard of high-grown greats who could be playing—and excelling—anywhere in the world. Now in the 24-team NASL, there must be two Americans starting on each club. Within years, certainly, Americanization will not be mandated, it will just be.

Of course, a good number of superstars—foreign and American—could not be included. That alone says much about how far NASL soccer has come in little more than a decade. Here they are then, the greats of NASL soccer— soccer's superstars.

FRANZ BECKENBAUER

In Europe he was called the "Kaiser," but after one season in the NASL, Franz Beckenbauer, 32, has become the commander-in-chief of the entire soccer world. The handsome West German joined the New York Cosmos at the peak of his powers and has completely lived up to his reputation. And what a reputation he had. Franz captained a World Cup winning team, three European Cup winners, one World Cup championship team, one European championship team, and two West German national championship teams (Bayern-Munich). He played for his national team 120 times and won numerous personal prizes, including the 1974 European Football Player of the Year award.

Besides his championships and medals, Franz captured the admiration of soccer players and fans alike for changing the very nature of the game. As a hugely successful offensive-minded defenseman, he forced soccer coaches around the world to rethink their tactics and strategies. He gave soccer a badly needed face-lift, and now he's in America to shape up the already improving game here.

How did the NASL, and the Cosmos in particular, land such a prize? The story is nearly as intriguing as Franz's playing. Signing Franz was a long, delicate process, a cross between a James Bond spying scheme and a round of Mideast negotiations. When the Cosmos were on tour in Europe in 1976, team President Clive Toye and then-Cosmos

Coach Gordon Bradley made their first real effort to get Franz. As Toye tells it: "We went to the hotel where the Bayern team was staying, a lovely little country inn. There was a team talk going on, so we waited. Then Bayern Coach Dettmar Cramer came out and did a double take when he saw us. We had lunch with Dettmar and we gradually brought the subject around to players, then around to Beckenbauer. We didn't get punched in the nose. We set things up for Gordon to spend some time with the club to study their operations. Gordon later spent three weeks with the club and saw a lot of Beckenbauer in action. He came back and said, 'Well, there's only one thing wrong with Beckenbauer—he makes a mistake about once every 400 times he touches the ball'—he was just overwhelmed by his ability, his professionalism and his attitude."

The initial talks at least served the purpose of convincing Bradley that a serious offer for Beckenbauer would be considered. Bradley returned to New York in November with the club's and Beckenbauer's asking price. Though it has never been revealed, it was reasonable enough for Toye to go to Munich in December with one of Warner Communications' financial officers to begin negotiations in earnest. There had already been the occasional squib in the German press that Beckenbauer was being courted by foreign soccer powers—actually the Spanish and the Argentinians were considered the major threats—so the Cosmos officials took every precaution to operate in secrecy to avoid the expected avalanche of national criticism in Germany. "With absolute efficiency," says Toye, "we were told to go to the hotel and they would telephone us at 11 o'clock."

Bayern's Robert Schwan called right on the hour; the negotiations were shifted into high gear. Says Toye: "We didn't want anyone coming to the hotel, so it was arranged that at exactly 12 o'clock on a corner across the street, down the road,'round the bend, a blue Mercedes would pull up, and Franz would be there to take us to his house outside of Munich. That was exactly what happened, and we sat there and began to talk around the problems. Mrs. Cramer came along to help us with interpreting—and to avoid being seen twice in one day in Franz's car, she drove us to a taxi stop and we took a cab back to the hotel.

"We had another meeting the next day—we took a taxi to a point in the woods near the Cramer's house, got out in the middle of all the cold and the snow, and ran 50 yards down the road to where Mrs. Cramer was waiting in her car to take us to Franz's house again."

After a brief return to New York, where the Beckenbauer deal got dubbed the Lou Gehrig Project to protect its secrecy, Toye and Bradley returned to Munich. Recalls Toye: "A group of us—Beckenbauer and his wife, Cramer and his wife, Schwan, Gordon and I—had lunch and we discussed all sorts of things like schools in New York, living accommodations and so on. I remember that lunch because we were all impressing on each other the need for absolute secrecy. Schwan said, 'Well, nobody knows about this except you and you . . .' and he went around the table one by one. When he finished, Franz added, 'And the waiter'—who had just left the room."

On Christmas Eve contracts were taken to Munich by special courier and Schwan called the next morning to confirm their arrival and said that they were already being carefully studied. After one more trip to Munich in January, Toye believed that most of the details in the contracts had been worked out.

He remained confident that the signing was imminent, until March 3, when Beckenbauer wired him with a simple message—the deal was off. Franz had finally told his plans to Bayern President Wilhelm Neudecker and the West German national team coach, Helmut Schoen. They and Franz's teammates put tremendous pressure on him not to leave his country with the '78 World Cup approaching. Franz was offered the national team coaching post once Schoen retired. The temptations to stay in Munich were great.

But Toye had been through the same kind of off-and-on

negotiations with Pele, so instead of giving up, he lay low
for a few weeks and returned to Munich later in the month.
By then, Beckenbauer was beginning to return to his decision to play with the Cosmos; the protests and pressure
over his plans had unnerved him but failed to irrevocably
change his mind. Toye made yet another trip to Munich
and began to go through the contracts again until it seemed
that the only way to answer all of Franz's questions was to
have him come to New York for a quick look-see. To avoid
the German press corps, which had learned about the res-
ervations Franz and Schwan made, they came a week
earlier than scheduled. After a complete physical examina-
tion by the Cosmos' doctors, Cosmos officials took Franz
for a helicopter ride over Manhattan and out to the Meadowlands. If Franz needed any further convincing, the chop-
per ride provided it.

Late in April, Toye made his sixth and final trip to
Munich—this time to negotiate the transfer fee that the
Cosmos would have to pay Bayern for Franz. Says Toye:
"That was not pleasant, Neudecker got up several times
and threatened to leave the meeting; he even put his coat
on once. He was constantly interrupting the proceedings—
and he doubled the price on us. We had been told that it
would be 1 million deutsch marks, now he was asking for
2.5 million." Finally, agreement was reached in principle,
lawyers were left to draw up the contracts, and arrange-
ments were made to meet in Lucerne for the final dis-
cussions. At those, it was made publicly official for the first
time—Franz would play his last game for Bayern–Munich
on May 21, and would be in New York to sign his new
contract four days later.

Although he was sure it was the right decision, leaving
Germany was a wrenching experience for Franz. Said he:
"The Saturday before I had to fight to keep my composure.
On the trip to play against Monchengladbach, I, as usual,
sat alone in the seat behind the bus driver. I needed the
concentration before this game more than usual. In the
locker room, I put on my Bayern jersey for the last time.

" 'The last time,' " that was the thought I was fighting in the stadium. It seemed to me that the public had never been so friendly, as if I had never understood my teammates better. The cheers as I left the stadium aroused emotion in me, but I didn't want to allow it to be noticed. In the locker room, it was like after every other game. I sat on the bench, while the others already had changed. I needed these minutes of relaxation as much as the time to concentrate before the game. One after another my teammates came by to shake my hand. 'Take care,' 'do well,' 'hang in there!' they said. I packed my equipment and left, as usual the last one out.

"Outside, Repp Senn, who had looked after the players' shoes, waited for me. He did that when I first came to the Bayern team 19 years before. The almost 80-year-old Sepp had known me since I was 13. He said, "It's already tragic, Franz."

Through more than six months of talks with the Cosmos, Franz could have pulled out of the deal many times, but even the outrage in Germany was not enough for him to stay. There were clearly many reasons why Franz was so intent on playing for the Cosmos. After his arrival in New York, Franz explained his motivations for the move. "First, of course, there was the good contract with Warner Communications and the Cosmos. Second, my age, I will be 32 in September and I was thinking that maybe in the U.S. I could play longer than in Europe because the season here would not be so hard. Third, the Cosmos had great players—Pele, Chinaglia and Ramon Mifflin. For me Pele is the greatest player I have ever seen in the world and I am proud to play on the same team with him."

Born on September 11, 1945, Franz grew up in a working class section of Munich. He got his first taste of soccer from hanging around with his brother who was five years older. Of his brother's role in his development as a soccer player, Franz says, "When he played football with his friends on the street, I begged to be allowed to play also. When the youths, all at least a head taller than me, needed one more, I was the last one chosen. I had incredible respect for my brother and his friends. Yet somehow I noticed that I was better technically than they were."

If Franz's brother grudgingly allowed him to join the street games, Franz's father made it even tougher for him to practice his game. Says Franz: "When my father, who worked in the main post office, came home at night, there was often a storm. He looked at my shoes, which I had been playing football in, and threatened that I should run around barefoot in the future. He said I should do my school work instead of ruining my shoes. His anger impressed me, but I never lost a chance to play football."

Still, Franz at first did not see himself as a pro soccer prospect. "When I left school after eight years, when I was 14 years old," he recalls, "it seemed sure that I would become a worker or an apprentice like my classmates. My favorite subject in school had been arithmetic and what attracted me most was being a salesman. So I became an apprentice at Alliance Insurance. They had never before hired somebody with my education, but they took me—I don't know why. I became the youngest member of the insurance company without even knowing what a premium was. Within three years my job was to arrange certain policies for customers. Actually I could be proud of myself. I already earned almost as much as my father and had achieved more than any of my classmates."

But Franz's career in the business world would be short-lived. The lure of his favorite sport had its influence, for sure, but there were other considerations. Says Franz: "Suddenly it struck me when I was 18 years old that I could already predict my life. I knew where I, with my limited education, would end up in the insurance hierarchy. My other self rebelled against my previously phlegmatic self. Against the advice of my father and acquaintances, I ignored my profession and concentrated more and more on football."

In Munich, there were two teams—fierce rivals—where Franz would likely play. Franz tells of his entry into the big leagues: "The youth division of the association where I learned the game was being dissolved. It was decided that the talented ones would go to the Munich 1860 team. In our working class neighborhood, we were all '60s fans, while the Bayern team got our utmost contempt."

But Franz's preference soon changed. "In one of our last games, we played against the school boys from 1860. My opponent guarding me was a hard, large boy named Bavernfeind. Just about every second, he would shout obscene words to me that had to do with my slight build. After I dribbled through his feet and shot a goal, he hit me when the referee's back was turned. I didn't hit back, but for me it was decided. I would never play on the same team as this boy. Against the advice of all my friends, I went to the 1860's archrivals, Bayern–Munich."

Franz developed quickly as a back on Bayern's youth squad and managed to keep his job at the insurance company. Then disaster struck. Recalls Franz: "At work, I got to know an older girl. Or rather, she got to know me. She was called Ingrid, I thought she was incredibly beautiful, and she helped me get over my shyness about girls. One day she overwhelmed me with the news that she was expecting a child by me. The trainer of the Bayern youth team somehow found out my private affairs and he threw me off the team.

"The world was destroyed for me. I firmly decided to give up football, yet, while I contemplated how I should make my exit from Bayern–Munich, I trained like a mad man. Every free minute I spent on the football field, often totally alone. I played the ball from head to foot and back; I practiced goal shots and flanks. My girl friend had the child, my son Thomas, of whom today I'm very proud. And I was accepted again into the first youth team of Bayern–Munich." It was about at the same time that Franz's superiors at Alliance Insurance finally had enough with his dual life. Either football or insurance, they said. After what he had just gone through, the decision was pretty easy for Franz. Full-time football it was.

Franz's prodigious talents first came to worldwide attention during the 1966 World Cup in England. At the same time that he displayed his many skills, not the least of which is his uncanny ability to make truly difficult plays look as if they were second nature to him, Franz also became the center of a growing controversy. "The Golden Boy" as he was known in his early days with Bayern–Munich has all the virtues of a great midfielder. He tackles superbly, can organize play while falling back on defense, has the know-how to create attacks from a position of depth, and is a dangerous shooter and passer when on the offensive.

With Bayern–Munich, he was used as a regular fullback with only his defensive talents employed. In Germany many fans pointed to the team's success as proof that he belonged in the back.

In the '66 World Cup, in which Germany lost the final to England in overtime, 4–2, Beckenbauer played midfield, and his job in the match was to shadow Bobby Charlton, England's star middie. Franz did it well, but while he neutralized Charlton, he himself was neutralized. Many of the world press at the game thought that Franz's role was misconceived—that as a back who could move up to the attack or as a midfielder without the prime responsibility to mark Charlton, he could have been a bigger offensive threat.

At the time, and to this day, Franz prefers to let others argue about where he should play. "The truth is that I love football," he says diplomatically, "and it does not matter whether I am told to play in midfield or in the back line. I like both roles equally well and enjoy playing just the same whatever the position."

At the next World Cup in Mexico, West Germany was eliminated in the semifinal game against Italy. Franz injured his shoulder during regulation time and during the overtime, when Italy outscored the Germans 3–2, could not play at full strength. Had he done so, many believe the outcome of the 30 minutes of pure offensive soccer would have been quite different.

In Mexico, Franz played both fullback and halfback, but the role that he was making increasingly his own was that of "libero" or free back. It was the Italian great, Giacinto Fachetti, who first used the free back idea successfully in the middle '60s, but he was mainly used to fill any gap that might develop in front of him. Thus, the term "sweeper" came into the game.

Beckenbauer saw the position in a different manner. Not assigned to man-to-man coverage on any of the opposing team's attackers, Franz exploited his freedom by playing both behind and in front of his defense. With an uncanny perception of the game, of what teammates are where, of what lines of attack are open or are about to be, what defensive weaknesses in position there may be, Franz made himself the total soccer player. Like hockey defenseman Bobby Orr, who turned his position into a greater offensive threat, Franz's adaptation of the free back's role to his own immense abilities transformed much of soccer strategy.

For Franz the whole field is his turf. When the moment is right, he'll leave defensive backline position and either dribble the ball all the way up field himself or draw more than one of the opponents to him and lay the ball off to one of his free teammates. A marvelous passer, Franz was particularly dangerous with Bayern–Munich when he worked the give-and-go · play with star forward Gerd Muller. Muller, who played especially well with his back to the opponent's goal, and Beckenbauer became the most feared combination in European football.

Unlike English teams whose play is characterized by extremely tight guarding, the German philosophy is to ignore such a formal approach and to allow the game itself to dictate the moves of the players. Thus, Franz was given wide latitude in each game to match his play to the circumstances at the time.

To the untrained eye, West German teams give the impression of fluidity, and at times, general confusion, with players running this way and that to no apparent purpose. But in fact, within the confusion are to be found intricate and precise maneuvers, especially when the teams go on the attack. The trouble with the strategy, if there is one, is essentially the same problem that can unravel an army's offensive in battle—if one little piece of machinery fails to function precisely as intended, the whole campaign breaks down in chaos. One longtime observer of West German soccer explains: "On a bad day, when the split-second timing required to make the strategy work fails, the German team can literally be destroyed by any second-rate team playing tight man-to-man defense, such as the Eastern European and English teams favor."

Since Germans view the game as such a complex undertaking, some of the negative reaction there to Franz's leaving was directed not at him but at the long reach of the NASL. Dr. Wilfried Gerhardt, a spokesman for the West German Football Federation, said, "The Americans are trying to begin at the top instead of being patient and starting at the bottom. Too many imports will hinder rather than help the growth of soccer in America." One NASL star scoffed at that idea. Said Pele: "You still need players like Beckenbauer to come into the league because there is more to learn."

Another Cosmo, however, had his own reasons for not favoring Franz's coming. "What is the use of Beckenbauer to us?" the outspoken striker Georgio Chinaglia wanted to know. "He's a great player, don't get me wrong. But is he going to help us with the crowds? No. He won't draw in this country. He will draw in tours overseas but not in this country. I don't live on the moon; I live in America. If Beckenbauer could bring more people to the stadiums in America I would buy 10 of him." But not for the same price, Chinaglia added. "Investing that much money in Beckenbauer is a bad idea for three reasons: First, because it is a lot of money. Second, because I don't think the man plans to remain in the U.S. and pass on his skills to American youth. And finally, because with that kind of money I could build three teams."

Most of the Cosmos, however, looked forward to

playing with Franz. Said Dave Clements: "The status of the players on the team will rise along with the status of the team." Added Bobby Smith: "The more stars I play with, the more my stock rises. I think Beckenbauer can help any team in the world." Perhaps happiest about getting Franz was Cosmos Coach Bradley. Said he: "Beckenbauer knows everything that goes on on the field. He does the full sweeper's job, but all of a sudden he'll take the ball and go on attack, too, and that's what makes him so thrilling. All of a sudden he'll make the break. He'll be off and running. I've seen him go through a whole team." For a purely personal reason, Bradley was doubly happy to have Franz. "Some day I'll be able to say that I coached the greatest offensive player who ever played and the greatest defensive player. This is history being made."

It began in the Meadowlands of New Jersey on May 25, 1977—the first day that Franz practiced with his new team. German-speaking defenseman Werner Roth was supposed to pick Franz up at his Manhattan hotel at 9:30 and drive him out to Giants Stadium. At 9:35 the Cosmos' office got a call. "Where is he?" Franz wanted to know. "I was five minutes late," said Roth, "and all hell broke loose. It was bedlam. Apparently he likes to be on time. After practice he said to me, 'You know something, I didn't miss much.' "

In fact, Franz was most interested in trying out the AstroTurf at the stadium and the Cosmos just wanted him to meet the press and the paparazzi from a half-dozen soccer-playing nations. As for the carpet he'd be playing many of his games on, Franz thought it would be "difficult because the ball moves so fast." Goalkeeper Shep Messing noted Franz's problem with it but thought he was already on the way to solving it. Said Messing: "His trademark is supposed to be the real long kick, but I think he found out that's going to be rough on the fast artificial turf. But this is a guy who can adjust. He brought 16 pairs of shoes over here with him. I heard he got held up at customs on account of them. Then when he came out to practice he was wearing exactly the right pair for the AstroTurf. We've been looking for shoes like that for years, and he brings them here from Europe."

Franz also brought a modest, low-key manner for dealing with the newsmen. Asked about his early days in soccer, he related how at first he was a big scorer. "Our team was always the best," he said. "Once, when I was 14, we beat a team 25–0. I scored 17 goals." But when he was 18, he added, he filled in at sweeper and fell in love with the position. "I like to see everything going on in front of me," he said. Then a New York journalist asked Cosmos General Manager Mike Martin to put Franz's talents into the American football idiom. "He's like a safetyman who intercepts passes and runs 'em back all the way, right?" the newsman said. "He's like a great punt and kick return man." Responded Martin: "He'll come on the safety blitz, too."

Four days after his first practice with the Cosmos, Franz had his debut in the league against the Tampa Bay Rowdies. At the time, the Rowdies led the Eastern Division with six wins against three losses, while the Cosmos were in third place, behind Fort Lauderdale, having lost four of their first nine games. More than a battle for first place, the match represented a milestone for the league. Perhaps in no other soccer event in history had so many brilliant players gathered on one field for a match. For New York, of course, there was Pele, Chinaglia, and now Beckenbauer. For Tampa Bay, Rodney Marsh, Derek Smethurst, and Stewart Jump led the parade. To see this supermatch, 45,288 fans jammed into Tampa Stadium, and millions more watched the nationally and internationally televised game.

The game, played in 86-degree sunshine, was all Tampa Bay's. The Rowdies overwhelmed the Cosmos, 4–2, spoiling Franz's special day. "We really psyched ourselves up to beat them," said rookie forward Steve Wegerle, who scored two goals for the Rowdies. "Everything in the papers all week has been about Beckenbauer and the Cosmos, so we had to show 'em and we did."

What the Rowdies did was come out, as Chinaglia said, "like lions." After the Cosmos missed a terrific opportunity when a Pele–Beckenbauer combination reached Chinaglia in the box, only to be headed just wide of the net, the Rowdies scored their first goal in the twentieth minute. Within three minutes, they scored another one as the Cosmos' chaotic defense failed to clear a corner kick and Ian Anderson's shot rolled through a number of legs into the goal. With one more Tampa Bay goal before the half, the Cosmos retreated to the locker room all but beaten.

In the second half, Tampa Bay once more opened the scoring on a penalty kick by Marsh. Soon afterward, however, the Cosmos showed some life. Tony Field scored, Nelsi Morais hit the right post, and Pele had a goal called back because of an offside call. Then finally, Franz had his moment. Taking a rebound in front of the Rowdies' netminder Paul Hammond, he booted in his first NASL goal.

After the embarrassing team effort, Franz, who had played splendidly, said: "Tampa really deserved to win because they put a lot of pressure on us. I had a lot of problems with the heat. I caught more wind in the second half, but I had difficulty in the first half breathing. Also, I had difficulty covering players because in West Germany we play man-to-man while here you switch and have to move around more. I was happy to score my first goal as a Cosmos player, but I would have rather had the team win."

But what had gone wrong with the Cosmos? Pele thought that there had been too many switches in the team's defensive lineup. Said he: "It was a mistake to take right full back and put him on the left. It shakes up the team too much. Second half was better. But it was 3–0 then and it's difficult to turn over a score like that." Added Tampa Bay Coach Eddie Firmani: "The Cosmos have players with individual ability, but have not quite put it together yet. They seemed to be jammed up at midfield."

Ironically, Firmani, himself, would get a chance to get the Cosmos together. Five days after the Rowdies crushed the Cosmos, he abruptly resigned, citing "personal reasons." In fact, the coach had been at odds with Tampa Bay's management over personnel issues. Within a month, Firmani was hired by the Cosmos to replace Bradley.

By the middle of July, Firmani switched Franz from sweeper to midfield. Said the coach: "Franz is wasted at sweeper. How can you play that talent at the back? He's the greatest distributor of the ball in the game." Franz had not played the position for seven years and had mixed feelings about the switch. On the one hand, he was not too pleased with the Cosmos' defensive set-up. Said Franz: "Werner Roth plays man for man the way I do, but the Brazilians, Nelsi and Rildo, play zone. So they don't follow their wingers when they come inside and it seems I am always guarding somebody. I am used to being more free." On the other hand, Franz saw some drawbacks about playing midfield. "The other teams are not stupid," he said. "If I am in midfield maybe they put a man to guard me 90 minutes and then what can I do?"

Simply play his best soccer of the season. In his second game at the position, before 34,189 fans at Giants Stadium, Franz scored twice and assisted on another goal in an 8–2 rout of the Washington Diplomats. He could not conceal his delight: "I can remember very easy the last time I scored two goals. It was last year in Munich. It's not too often I score two goals in a game." Perhaps, but Franz played two more dazzling games at midfield as the regular season closed and then helped to lead the Cosmos through the playoffs and the 2–1 championship victory over Seattle.

For his outstanding play throughout the season Franz was named the league's Most Valuable Player. He narrowly edged out Pele by 282 to 276 votes. Said Franz: "It's a tremendous honor for me. I have won many awards in my career, but to win something like this in my first full season here is very meaningful."

Maybe even more so, given Franz's assessment of the NASL, which he made midway through the season. Said he: "I can now compare soccer here with the game in Europe, and I must say that soccer in the States is very, very good. In Germany and the rest of Europe people have the wrong opinion that soccer in the U.S. is no good, that it is not fast and not hard. And people in America think that soccer in Europe is all great. That is not true either. I know soccer. For the last 13 years I have been in all parts of the world and have played against the best teams. So I can compare, and for me most of the teams in the NASL can play in any league anywhere." For that matter, Franz Beckenbauer could by the M.V.P. anywhere. Indeed, the Kaiser has already conquered two continents.

EUSEBIO

Eusebio Da Silva Ferreira, better known to soccer fans simply by his first name, is the one man in the game who has ever been compared to the King. And it is not something that the so-called "Portuguese Pele" relishes. After the 1966 World Cup thrust Eusebio into the limelight with his smashing nine-goal performance, he said, "I feel calling me the new Pele is very unfair, for both Pele and me. To me, Pele is the greatest soccer player of all time. I only hope that one day I can be the second-best ever."

Besides being unfair to Eusebio, the comparison always caused a vexing problem at home. Eusebio's mother loved to see her son's name in the papers, but since she could not read very well, seeing Eusebio referred to as a new Pele only confused matters for her.

There is no confusion, though, about why Eusebio has had to endure the comparison. An altogether electrifying forward, with a booming shot and speed that reflects his preferred nickname, "The Black Panther," Eusebio is, behind Pele, the highest scoring player in the history of soccer and stands alone with the best goals per game average.

Interestingly, the two superscorers share similar backgrounds. While Pele grew up in poverty in the tiny town of Tres Coracoes in Brazil and kicked a rag-stuffed sock around to practice, Eusebio, a year younger, kicked a ball in the narrow paths of Lourenco Marques, a poor town in the Portuguese East African colony of Mozambique. As Pele's dad couldn't afford to buy a ball for his son, Eusebio's family was poor enough to let him play without shoes.

That explains the delight Eusebio felt when, as a ten-year-old, he found an old worn out soccer boot in a garbage dump. To him, it was the most beautiful thing he had ever set his eyes upon, and he immediately laced it on. The boot was at least a couple of sizes too big, so Eusebio just carried it around with him—wherever he went. When his bare shooting foot would swell up from smashing the ball, Eusebio would put on the boot and loop the laces under his foot so that it would fit.

Pele was given a handful of gold coins when he signed his first professional contract at age 15; Eusebio's bonus when, at the same age, he signed with the Sporting Club of Lourenco Marques was more practical. Eusebio remembers that "money didn't mean anything to me at that time. I was just happy to get, as my bonus, my first pair of soccer boots."

Eusebio's wizardry for the Mozambique team soon became widely reported in Portugal, and he was offered a position with Lisbon's famous Benfica team. But there was a problem still to be surmounted. The Sporting Club Lourenco Marques was a farm team of sorts of the Sporting Club of Portugal and a legal battle flared up over which of the Lisbon teams Eusebio should play for.

When the legal dust settled in May 1961, Eusebio became a Benfica player and his path to greatness was finally cleared. Eusebio's first full stride down that path came during the summer, when Benfica played in a tournament in Paris. At the time of the four-team competition, Eusebio was not yet a starting player, but the final game turned that situation around. Losing to Santos of Brazil, 5–0, with Pele the dominant force in the game, the Benfica manager, with twenty minutes remaining, put in his young, inexperienced substitute. Incredibly, Eusebio destroyed the Santos defense. Completely outshining Pele, he put in three goals, and though Santos added another score to make the final tally 6-3, it was the rookie's hat trick that everyone marveled over. With that one game, Eusebio had set a firm foundation for his building reputation.

Over the next five years, Eusebio's talents became all too well appreciated by Benfica's opponents. Although he had to undergo a number of knee operations, Eusebio repeatedly ranked among the top scorers on the continent. Among his greatest attributes, Eusebio's speed is said to be what sets him apart from other accomplished players. As a 16-year-old he was clocked at under eleven seconds in the 100-meter dash, and he would later remark on the importance of his speed to his overall play. Said Eusebio: "Sprinting has always been an important part of my life, and I am convinced that my speed has made all the difference between success and failure. Too few people in the game realize the value of speed properly used. It isn't just a case of speed for speed's sake, or of running fast, but the speed at which you can do things." By that, Eusebio means that while most professional players have mastered the various skills of the game—dribbling, passing, trapping, heading, shooting, only the great ones perform such tasks quickly enough to make them brilliant maneuvers.

A description of Eusebio in action by one long-time observer of the game in Europe makes clear just how "The Black Panther" utilizes his speed: "He will lope around the field, face expressionless, arms dangling, but the brain ticking. Suddenly he springs into action. He has made yards before anyone realizes he has moved at all, and many have been the times when people have complained about Eusebio being left unmarked when, in fact, he has, in a split second, made the space in which to operate. He does nothing slowly, but equally so he does nothing at the same pace. When he is dribbling, he constantly varies his pace, and from a standing start he can reach top speed in such a short time, you think he has been propelled out of starting blocks.

"To watch him charming the ball down the pitch is one

of the great sights of football. Tantalizingly varying his pace, he will cleverly slide his body between the ball and the challenger should any defender get too near, and you can always expect him to strike quickly by doing the unexpected.

Just that happened when the sixteen top national teams met in England for the 1966 World Cup. The championship, held for the most part at the famed Wembley Stadium, will be remembered as one of the most disputed and brutal World Cups in history. The refereeing was at best spotty, and flagrant fouls marked many of the contests. The crowds in England, well accustomed to a rough brand of soccer, reacted with uncharacteristic anger when such dirty play was exhibited, and some players, who would normally conduct themselves well within the rules, were almost forced to abandon their good sportsmanship at these times and retaliate in kind.

Brazil, a leading contender for the championship, was particularly hurt by the chippy tactics. In the opening round, they beat Bulgaria, 2–0, but not without paying an unestimable price. In the first half, Pele notched one of his team's goals on a free kick. Thenceforth, the close marking that Zhechev was giving him became ruthless shadowing that resulted in Pele being brutally tripped and then trampled. One French journalist, looking somberly down on the battleground from his seat in the Press Box, predicted, "Pele won't finish the World Cup. It's amazing he hasn't gone mad."

With Pele still recovering from the bruises he sustained at the feet of the Bulgarians, he was forced to sit out Brazil's game against Hungary, and Brazil bowed to its second Eastern European opponent, 3–1. In Brazil's last qualifying round against Portugal, the King tried to play again, but he was obviously not ready. All the more reason why soccer fans in England and around the world were shocked when, with the game firmly in Portugal's control, Pele was subjected to a violent double foul by Morais that put him out of the game. An overly indulgent English referee allowed Morais to stay in the game. Pele's replacement, Silva, had also been hurt, and so Portugal was playing against virtually a ten-man team.

After sixty-five minutes, Brazil cut Portugal's two-goal lead when Rildo, a young, speedy back, made a long run and scored. Twenty minutes later, however, Brazil's hopes were smashed when Eusebio took a right corner and booted the last goal home. Following the 3–1 loss for Brazil, there were reports that bridges in Rio de Janeiro and other cities in the country had to be closed because there were several suicides.

Eusebio would, after his sparkling World Cup performance, be able to empathize with Pele for being the target of such cheap shots. Though he himself has been criticized for playing what he calls "anti-football," Eusebio pleads not guilty on the grounds of self-defense. He is constantly aware that some defenders will try just about anything in an important game to stop him from scoring. He believes that because of his status in the game, the defenders are usually given the benefit of the doubt by referees. Says he: "Once I retaliated and was sent off, but nothing was done to the fellow who had been fouling me all the time."

Though Eusebio was able to commiserate with a superstar's special dilemma, it was Pele's injuries that helped enable Eusebio to step into the spotlight by himself. In the three qualifying games that Portugal played and won and scored nine goals, six of them were made by the Black Panther. Then, in the surprisingly dicey quarterfinal game against the underrated North Koreans, Eusebio's prowess was displayed in all its astonishing diversity. The Koreans came out strong on the attack and early in the game commanded a 3–0 lead. By half time, however, Portugal managed to cut its deficit by two goals. On the first, Simoes had a breakaway and coolly passed off to Eusebio who blasted the ball into the net. Three minutes before intermission, Torres was fouled inside the penalty area, and Eusebio's blistering penalty shot was too accurately placed in the right corner for the goalie to stop. After he scored, Eusebio quickly scooped up the ball and sprinted back to midfield to get the game going again. Incredibly, he was intercepted and upbraided by an outraged North Korean before play could resume.

Fifteen minutes into the second half, Eusebio struck once more. He dashed through the careless Koreans and knotted the match at 3-3, then shortly afterward, made one of his spirited left-wing runs, deaked defenders going in, and was finally chopped down for a penalty. Eusebio's penalty shot found the net. The North Koreans managed another tally, but the damage was complete. In an effort that was, to say the least, entertaining, the North Koreans had squandered their lead with a listless defense that was nearly as fascinating to watch as their swirling, daring attack at the match's beginning.

Eusebio would cap his magnificent World Cup performance in Portugal's semifinal game against England. Though he was shadowed incessantly by the tenacious Nobby Stiles and held practically shotless, Eusebio put the game within reach when he fooled Gordon Banks, the English goalkeeper, on a penalty shot with eight minutes remaining. Until the end, England held on to its 2-1 advantage by turning back Eusebio and his tireless teammates Coluna and Simoes with the fierce defensive play of Stiles, Bobby Moore, Jackie Charlton, and the faultless Banks. At the game's final whistle, Eusebio left the field weeping and the appreciative English crowd saluted him with a rousing ovation—a just reward for his unflagging desire throughout the competition and his remarkable six-goal performance.

Having captured the world soccer community's adulation for this play in England—in much the same way that he came to notice on the continent in the early sixties by leading Benfica to two consecutive European Cup titles—Eusebio was dubbed by many sportswriters to be the new

King of Soccer. While he protested vigorously that he was still solely heir-apparent, or the game's Prince, Eusebio could not stop the talk.

The debate over who was the greatest hardly had time to build before it was settled in a special international match between Pele's Santos team and Benfica. In the game at New York's Downing Stadium, Eusebio's American debut was spoiled by the heavyweight champ—Pele. As if he had to prove that the title still belonged unquestionably to him, Pele led Santos with a goal and three assists to a 4–0 victory. And as the one-sided match neared its end, Pele deftly stole the ball off Eusebio's foot, saluted the Portuguese star and sped off down the field to the wild applause of the 22,000 spectators. After the game, Eusebio put the flattering comparisons to Pele into perspective. "I told you not to discredit Pele," said Eusebio. "He's still as great as ever, and he'll stay that way until he decides to retire."

Eusebio continued to terrorize Benfica's European rivals until 1975. After a dispute with his club's management over salary, he signed with the Boston Minutemen of the NASL, the same team that had snared Eusebio's teammate Antonio Simoes. By mutual agreement, Eusebio's contract with the Minutemen was not renewed, and he moved to Toronto. There, he and West German star Wolfgang Suhnholz led the Canadian team to the NASL 1976 championship. During the regular season, Eusebio scored sixteen goals and in the final game of the championship series, he sparked Toronto with its first goal in the 3–0 victory over Minnesota.

Moving to his third team in North America in as many years, Eusebio signed with the Las Vegas Quicksilvers for the 1977 season. The team, formerly the San Diego Jaws, looked to Eusebio and Suhnholz, who they also acquired from Toronto, to give them a shot at the championship. The first game of the year, against the New York Cosmos, marked the twelfth meeting of Eusebio and Pele in their long careers. The Quicksilvers took the match, 1–0, but the only scores the King and the Prince made were with the press. Pele said that it was only the media that had built up the rivalry between the two, and that in fact, the two were good friends. Asked by one reporter to describe each other, Pele told of how he had tried to get his Santos club to pick up Eusebio after their teams met for the first time. Santos' president demurred, saying that Eusebio did not have enough experience. "Enough experience," Pele laughed. "He had three goals. I don't know why the president said no."

As for Pele, Eusebio, who is not as fluent in English as the Brazilian, nonetheless found the right word: "unique."

The rest of the season was not a happy one for Eusebio. Plagued by back and foot injuries, his playing time was greatly reduced. When he did play, he provided the young team with strong leadership, but suffered personally from a run of bad luck during which he repeatedly hit the goalpost on his shots. Finally, at midseason, Eusebio broke his unusual scoreless streak by scoring two goals in a game against the Connecticut Bicentennial.

With the King now retired, Eusebio is the leading scorer active in the game. The Prince no doubt will retire soon, but for at least one season, fans of the NASL will be able to see him sprinting past defenders and driving the ball into the net. Whenever it does happen, leaving the game will not be easy for Eusebio. "It flows through my veins, mixing with my blood," he once said. "Cut off football and you have cut off my life just as effectively as if you had stopped my heart."

ERIC MARTIN

What's the number one breeding ground for NASL goal-keepers? The coal mines of the United Kingdom, of course. In England, Gordon Banks bagged coal before turning his attention to the football pitch. And in Perth, Scotland, Eric Martin blackened his fingers in the mines before bloodying them in the goalmouth. Says the Washington Diplomat four-year veteran: "In my town, you either went into the mines or into the Army. It's very rare for a kid to turn pro out of the mines; maybe one in a hundred makes it. Every kid plays soccer there, but I was very lucky."

Lucky and awfully good. Eric left the mines after a year and a half at age 16. He quickly found his way to the Scottish first division, where he put in a pair of seasons. Then he moved on to England to tend goal for Southampton. He stayed there nine seasons and helped his club stay in the first division for seven of them. They were fine years, but at times the spotlight's glare was too much. Recalls Eric: "There is a lot more pressure in England, and it comes from all sides. The press, the public, everywhere. You can't walk down the street there without being recognized. If you've had a bad game, everyone lets you know about it. Let's face it, soccer is as big as American football is here."

The lower key atmosphere in America was just one thing that attracted Martin to the Dips. But there was another consideration—one that Eric feels is widely shared back home. Says he: "I'd say at least fifty percent of the players in England would like to come to America to play. The second, third, and fourth division players would especially like to come over, since most of them earn peanuts. It's a big opportunity here for most players."

Eric joined the Dips midway through the 1975 season. An outbreak of injuries left the club without strong goal-keeping, so Coach Dennis Viollet placed an overseas S.O.S. to Martin, who thought at the time that he was getting a short, stop-gap assignment. Says Eric: "I was here for six weeks and then I turned around and went back to England. I was going to play another season over there."

During his '75 stint, Eric played an impressive goal. Although the Dips narrowly missed the playoffs, Eric made them tough down the home stretch. In his ten games, he posted a 1.25 goals-against average and a shutout. Viollet was pleased enough with Eric to place another call to lure him back again.

It didn't take much persuading. "I like people here," Eric says, "and I was doing something I enjoyed." The Dips also knew that Eric would enjoy becoming an important part of the league's youth promotion program. Says Eric: "In those six weeks I had little time to notice much. But on returning, it was all around me, kids playing the game everywhere."

Eric's presence in the goal for the entire '76 season helped the Dips to make the playoffs for the first time. Unfortunately for the Dips, injuries again took their toll on the team's performance and were especially felt on defense where, during the latter part of the season, missed assignments led to too many opponents' goals. Of all the forwards that Eric had to face, the two toughest were Cosmo aces Pele and Georgio Chinaglia. Adds Eric: "Another lad who isn't noticed as much is George Best, a tremendous forward. And when he's turned on, Rodney Marsh is another incredible player. Give him a split second and he'll score."

During the off-season Eric stays in shape by playing in some informal amateur matches on Sundays and conducts many clinics for Washington-area youngsters. By working with the kids, Eric has a unique vantage point from which to judge the future of soccer in America. Says Eric: "Everybody's always saying it's ten years away. I say it's six. There'll be a problem soon when they try to choose a national team. There will be so many good players they won't know who to pick." Eric's advice to youngsters with goals (or saves) in their dreams: "They should play as much as possible. Every kid, no matter what country, needs the practice."

WILLIE MORGAN

The Chicago Sting was stung. In its first six games of the 1977 season, the team seemed listless, scored only three goals and picked up not one victory. Coach Bill Foulkes found the losing streak, the worst start in the Sting's three-year history, puzzling. "What is disturbing," he said, "is that we have better personnel than we had last year but we're not getting as much effort from them. The players realize they are not playing with the same enthusiasm they played with last season." All very reasonable, but in a less guarded moment Foulkes admitted that things were "getting desperate."

Enter Willie Morgan. The 32-year-old former captain of Manchester United had always been a strong offensive threat in his seventeen years of First Division soccer. A native of Glasgow, Scotland, he was instrumental in getting the Scottish National Team to the World Cup finals in Munich in 1974. He had also been considering offers from NASL teams before Foulkes, who had been his teammate for four years at Manchester United, finally landed him, just before the season began. Said Willie: "The fact that I knew Billy is why I came here. I've had people after me to come to the U.S. for a couple of years. I refused mainly because it was such a big step to agree to play for the whole summer. But Bill and Sting owner, Lee Stern sold the thing to me. They promised they'd take care of me and my family. It's nice to have someone to go to in case you need them."

And more than nice for the Sting to have someone like Morgan to turn to after their horrendous start. "When we arrived and I was told that the team had lost its first six games, my first thought was to get back on the plane," Willie said. "And I knew we had two of the hardest teams in the league to play next, so I was thinking we could be 0–8. It's hard to come in and have that pressure on you right away. You really don't expect it. Usually you can ease yourself in."

But Willie is an unusual player, and after only two practices with the team, during which time he quietly established himself as a field leader, he led the Sting to victories against those "hardest" rivals. At Soldier Field, where Willie had to quickly adapt to the queer things that AstroTurf can do to a soccer ball, he took charge almost from the opening whistle in the match against the high-scoring and division-leading Tampa Bay Rowdies. At the 6:32 mark, Willie came off a dazzling bit of footwork and lined a wicked shot into the net. Fourteen minutes later, Willie and Bill Jennings (an English standout at West Ham who also had just arrived in Chicago) teamed up for another score. Willie lofted a pass across the penalty area on a free kick, and Jennings nodded it past Rowdies' goalkeeper Paul Hammond. Then, with less than ten minutes left in the first half, Willie worked his magic again, faking a defender and driving home the Sting's third goal.

Tampa Bay, not about to play dead, answered twelve seconds later with an unassisted goal by Derek Smethurst. In the second half, with the Sting's defense getting sloppy, the Rowdies tied the game on a goal by Adrian Alston and another by Smethurst. But when Tampa Bay's Wes McLeod was called on a hand ball, on a shot by Willie, Midfielder Jim Kelly scored on the penalty shot, and the Sting held on to its slim lead for the remaining thirty minutes and finally had its first victory.

The losing streak snapped, the Sting took on the famous Cosmos two days later, and once more Willie played a major role, assisting on one goal and providing steady leadership for the young team that copped a 2-1 win. For his outstanding two-game debut, Willie became the NASL's offensive player of the week.

For Foulkes, Willie's superb effort altogether justified the faith he had in his new acquisition. After the Tampa Bay game, the coach beamed, "Morgan is just lethal out there," and added that with Jennings and striker Ron Moore on the attack, the trio made one of the best front lines in the league. On Willie's long-range worth to the club, Foulkes was just as effusive with his praise: "He's a leader on the field. He likes taking charge of things and it's very important we have someone who can do this. We've lacked this for three years."

Willie was fully aware of the responsibility that he had incurred. Explaining his style of leadership, he said, "I don't yell, I like to talk to people and encourage them, especially the young lads. It's vital at this stage in their careers that they have someone to talk to when things are going wrong. Basically, I think the team lacked confidence. They needed someone who could knit the team together. When you lose six matches in a row, it's hard to face each one. You don't want to go out and play anymore."

After the Sting's first two victories of the year, the whole outlook changed. Willie admitted that the team had a way to go and would not venture a prediction on its future success, but he did note some positive signs: "The players feel better. They are looking forward to playing again. The important thing is that the team is winning. From my own point of view, I expected to come out and play well, and I say that without meaning to be big-headed. Sometimes it isn't so difficult to play with a new team in football. You just go out and play."

After the two big victories against the Rowdies and Cosmos, the Sting went on to win two more of its next three games. The remainder of the season, however, was not as rewarding, as the Sting failed to reach the playoffs. Still, Willie Morgan, who had given up his favorite off-season activities—spending time with his family and playing tennis and golf—to help out his old buddy, Bill Foulkes, could be pleased with a job well done.

KYLE ROTE, JR.

He had already won three high school letters for baseball, basketball, and football. He was certain he would follow his famous father's lead and become a pro football player. He knew that he had all the physical abilities and mental quickness to make it. How then did Kyle Rote, Jr. become the first American soccer player of note in the North American Soccer League? It began, naturally enough, with his dedication to football. In the summer between his junior and senior years at the Highland Park High School in Dallas, Rote and a bunch of teammates from the football squad decided that they needed some kind of conditioning program to keep themselves fit through the summer. No sense staying in shape for the whole school year then losing it during the summer and having to work like a dog to get it back.

And so Kyle and friends turned to soccer. They formed a team, read a few books on the game, and studied the basic rules. At the time, the United Soccer Federation franchise of Dundee United played in Dallas, and some of the footballers went to a few games to get at least some feel for it. Doing all the sensible things to start up the group, the team needed only a name to make themselves a unit, if not a wholly respectable soccer club. Said Kyle: "What we initially lacked in finesse we made up for with our devastating team name—the Black Bandits." The handle grew from the group's respect for black athletes and their fascination with a bunch of football players at Louisiana State University—the Chinese Bandits. "We hoped," says Kyle, "the team name would scare the daylights out of other teams and give us a unique bond to rally around."

The Bandits coached themselves, and though about as awesome as a team of 150-pound Ping-Pong players, they did fairly well against the area prep schools they challenged. From one game to the next, Kyle's squad picked up some nuances, just as Little Leaguers, with a little help from their coaches, learned things like the sacrifice bunt or hit-and-run. The real boost for the team, however, came neither from within their own ranks nor from some overexcited father. One day, while the Bandits were practicing at the high school field, they were spotted by a passing motorist who could not help but stop his car and take a gander. The driver was Ron Griffith, sports columnist for a Scottish newspaper who was in Dallas covering the Dundee United team.

After a few minutes of watching all the mistakes that the Bandits were making on the field, Griffith, according to Kyle, "rushed over and in forty-five minutes of Lancashire dialect tried to cover the fine points of the game. At first we were offended by this guy with a funny accent who was butting in, but we soon discovered he knew what he was talking about. He explained that we should kick the ball off the side of the foot instead of the toe. He told us how to make the two-handed throw-in from the sidelines and even showed us the overhead scissors kick. We found out the game could be something more than a conditioner, but never in my wildest dreams did I think that I'd be playing professional soccer someday—in my hometown to boot."

Although the Bandits and Griffith sparked Kyle's interest in the game, it would still be a number of years before he devoted the kind of attention to soccer that would enable him to make it to the pros. Everything about his athletic career at Highland Park pointed to football. While he captained the basketball and baseball teams, Kyle excelled at quarterback and safety on the gridiron. By

graduation he had more than 50 college scholarship offers
from which to choose. It seemed virtually a certainty that
like Bobby Layne, Doak Walker, and his father before
him, Kyle would become one more Highland Park grad to
make it big in the NFL.

Choosing the right college became a matter of deciding
not only what school would provide the best atmosphere
for polishing his football skills, but would also provide the
kind of education that Kyle and his father had decided
would be essential for a career after his playing days were
over. One school that was eliminated for special reasons
was Southern Methodist. The Alma Mater of Kyle Sr.
wanted young Rote badly but the pitfall was obvious to
both Rotes. Says Kyle: "I don't think I was conscious of it
at the time, but having to fit into the mold of my father was
probably a decisive factor against the school. They even
promised me old number 44—one of the most famous
SMU jerseys. The comparison worried me. It was not only
the pressure of living up to the legend of a great football
player, but also trying to resurrect an era of SMU athletics
that had long since passed. That was a heavy load for an
eighteen-year-old kid."

Of all the recruiters pursuing Kyle, only those from
Oklahoma State University expressed as much interest in
Kyle's education as in the football program which was just
what Kyle wanted to hear. Says Kyle: "I had a deep desire
to do well scholastically. I knew that any big time sports
pursuit alone would be a very shaky foundation for the
future. I felt that Oklahoma State could provide me with
both. Only time would prove me wrong."

Not much time at that. Halfway through the freshman
football season, an option play Kyle ran as quarterback
during a practice session ended in disaster. Running later-
ally down the line, after taking the snap, Kyle saw a hole
open up; rather than pitching out to his running back, he
headed downfield. Then a teammate missed his blocking
assignment and crunched Kyle instead. The result: a broken femur and badly damaged ligaments in one knee. An

operation and physical therapy made the joint stronger than ever, but during his recuperation period, Kyle had time to give more thought to the kind of education he was getting at OSU. While there was nothing intrinsically lacking in the academic program, Kyle, shut off in the jock dorm among schoolmates who did not share his concern for studying, felt that he needed to be pushed more toward maintaining his interest in his prelaw courses. After consulting with his closest friend from Dallas and his high school basketball coach, Kyle decided to transfer to the University of the South in Sewanee, Tennessee.

As Kyle tells it in his autobiography, *Beyond the Goal,* "transferring was the best thing that ever happened to me. Little did I realize how much it would change my life. It was here that my view of academic life was broadened, my vocational goals took a new direction." Sewanee, an Episcopal church-related school, was as different from OSU as the verdant undulating countryside of Eastern Tennessee is from the Oklahoma prairie. Small, secluded, and hardly rah-rah, Sewanee allowed Kyle to pursue non-athletic interests, working for school publications and the campus radio station. Moreover, since he was no longer living solely with jocks, Kyle became exposed to different types of people than he had met at OSU. Living with English, forestry, medicine, and teaching majors sharpened Kyle's perspective on both himself and his generation.

The greater awareness of a world outside of sports may have been crucial in Kyle's switch to soccer. Says Kyle: "I had hopes to play both football and soccer, but it soon became apparent that was impossible. The seasons overlapped and I had to make a choice. I love football, but somehow there seemed a new challenge in soccer. I had already played collegiate football. I rationalized that I could always play football my last two years. So I chose soccer, purely for the job of playing the game."

Ironically, Kyle thought that when he left OSU's big time football program that he was virtually writing off a career as a professional athlete. Playing soccer at Sewanee was not exactly a ticket to the pros. If Kyle had given any thought to a pro soccer stint: "I never would have picked Sewanee. It does not give athletic scholarships and does not attract the super high school prospects. It has a solid program and is competitive within its own league, but it is not a soccer power by any means. However, it was soon evident that I was 'hooked' on the game."

Not that soccer playing at Sewanee was all fun. Although the school budgeted about $200,000 a year for the football squad, soccer was appropriated only $2,000. The soccer players felt that they were "neglected orphans of the athletic department," Kyle recalls. For example, although all the other school teams were provided equipment, the soccer players, who needed less than most of the other athletes, had to purchase their own shoes. Further, although Sewanee has plenty of land, the soccer team had to use the football practice field for its own games. Since football tends to tear up a field about as much as fans in New York do after championship victories by the Mets or Yankees, the soccer team never had the smooth surface that the game requires.

What Sewanee did have going for its soccer program was Coach Mac Petty. Though he had never played or coached soccer, Petty crash-coursed his way into gaining the respect of Kyle and his teammates. Says Kyle: "He is one of the few coaches I have seen who had little temper, was happy-go-lucky, and yet could have discipline. He was a positive reinforcer. Many coaches are neutral or even negative reinforcers who try to achieve discipline by scolding, cajoling, or threatening. Coach Petty was positive and constructive. He was extremely perceptive and adaptable. He probably did as much as anyone in helping me to keep sports in proper perspective."

Sewanee also put Kyle's love life in order. Mary Lynne Lykins, one of the first women admitted to the traditionally all-male Sewanee, met Kyle while they were sophomores and they quickly developed an intense, yet "open," relationship with each other. They seem particularly compatible in their views on the importance of religion, of discussing the subject during long walks after evening chapel services. Married the day after graduation, they continued their commitment to God by jointly teaching Sunday school. As Kyle says, "There is nothing more important in life than a solid spiritual foundation."

Mary Lynne and Kyle set up their first home in a small Dallas apartment; thanks, to a great degree, to the local NASL team, the Tornados. The night before the league's 1972 draft, Tornado General Manager Joe Echelle called Kyle in Sewanee and surprised him with "We're thinking of drafting you in the first round tomorrow. I just called to make sure you knew who we are and that you'd consider playing professional soccer with us." When word came the next day that the Tornado had indeed picked Kyle, the decision was an easy one for him. A major factor, of course, was his being able to play in his hometown.

While the Tornado had followed Kyle's progress in soccer at Sewanee, the team management was swayed mostly by the obvious fan appeal that having a Rote on the field would engender. His selection was a risk but not a blind one. Tornado Coach Ron Newman clearly remembered an afternoon in the summer of '69 that seemed to make the gamble worth taking. The Black Bandits scrimmaged the Tornado, and Newman recalls, "Kyle didn't look too polished, just big and strong. Then at one point the fellow who was marking him eased off just a little. Bang. Kyle was by him like a shot and positively cannoned the ball into the back of our net. Well, I thought, one goal might be a fluke. Then a few minutes later he did the same thing again. It was a pretty impressive performance. When his name came up in the draft, it was not hard to remember that tremendous potential."

Whatever Coach Newman's recollections, Kyle's new teammates were less than impressed with his efforts at his first practice. Remembers Kyle: "It was just horrible because there's so much difference between the college and pro game. Anyway, while I was in the shower after the scrimmage I heard my teammates saying to each other, 'He'll never make it. He's just terrible.' " Only goalkeeper Kenny Cooper came to Kyle's defense, challenging anyone to bet his week's salary that Kyle wouldn't make it. No one took Cooper up on the wager.

Needless to say, Kyle did make it, but at first it was more his attitude than his skill that enabled him to stick—and, of course, the Tornado's desire to get a box office draw on the field. According to Kyle, his willingness to learn from his teammates, particularly the soccer-sophisticated foreigners, made up for his lack of refined ability. At each practice, Kyle would ask one of his mates to take fifteen minutes after the formal session to work on one facet of the game. Eighteen-year veteran John Best gave Kyle pointers on heading, and Brazilian Luiz Juracy taught him the technique of always moving with intense muscular control. Then all-league goalie Ken Cooper discussed the types of shots that netminders find most difficult to stop and midfielder Bob Ridley demonstrated one of them—the top-spin shot that, if hit right, dips and skids past the goalie.

The extra hours of practice, as well as his teammates' unselfish tutelage, began paying dividends as soon as the Tornados opened the 1973 season at Texas Stadium. For the joust against the Toronto Metros, 19,343 soccer nuts endured a downpour and were justly rewarded for their resolve. With the artificial turf so waterlogged that it was like playing on a sponge, Kyle took a curving pass from Mike Renshaw on the right wing with a diving header and popped the rain-heavy ball into the net. The dive onto the wet field had Kyle sliding eight feet; he recalls thinking at the time, "If that ball doesn't go in I'm just going to keep right on sliding up the ramp and into the dressing room." Assisting on another goal, Kyle was voted the star player of the game—an honor that brought two free pairs of slacks. "That was like a week's salary for me," says Kyle, who was drawing the less than subsistence-level annual salary of $1,400 a year.

After spending most of his rookie year on the bench, the

'73 season, from the Toronto game onward, was another matter. Coach Newman spent most of Kyle's first season developing him into a target man, probably the easiest position on a soccer club that can be taught. What impressed Newman about Kyle's potential as a goal area forward was his ability to jump. Says Newman: "He could get off the ground like you'd think he was never coming down again. I thought we'd have to train him to come down quicker so he could get back into the game." When Newman began starring Kyle in '73, the coach recalls that "a lot of people thought I was doing it as a gimmick, but I wasn't. He deserved his place. That first year he did very well. He had this thing a lot of goalscorers have; they get a lot of luck, the ball always seems to be bouncing in front of them." Indeed, Kyle's first full season in the league was full of fortunate opportunities. After splitting a number of early close games, the Tornado began rolling at midseason in a game against the St. Louis Stars. As it happened, Kyle started the contest picking pines: on the bench, that is. Newman felt that Kyle had lost confidence in himself, that he had begun to press so as not to make any mistakes. But when midfielder Bobby Ridley twisted his knee and had to be taken out with 20 minutes left in the game, Kyle had a chance to get back in Newman's favor. At the 76-minute mark, a St. Louis defender tried to head the ball away from his goal, but it fell at Kyle's feet, and he booted it past goalie Mike Winter to break the scoreless tie. Then with 2:20 remaining, Kyle and Ilija Mitic went on the attack. Working a perfect give-and-go, Kyle drew the defense to him and slipped a pass off to Mitic. From a dozen yards out, Mitic put away the clinching goal just inside the near post.

The 2–0 victory put the Tornado on track to the playoffs. It also put Kyle back into the starting lineup. Given the opportunity, he wasn't about to squander it. Going into the last regular season game, Kyle had amassed 28 points with 9 goals and 10 assists. To win the league scoring title—Wareen Archibald of Miami had taken a one-point lead the night before—Kyle needed a goal or two assists. With fifteen minutes left in the game, Luiz Juracy was knocked down in the penalty box and the Tornado was awarded a penalty kick. Normally, Mitic would have taken it, but the team wanted to give Kyle a chance to top Archibald. Kyle promptly booted it home and walked off with the scoring title. Says Kyle: "I was elated at winning the crown, but I also knew that I could not have done it without the help of my teammates. They were simply fantastic. After all the time they spent working with me, it was their scoring title too."

In the playoffs, Kyle continued his scoring skein. In a 1–0 win over the Cosmos, he scored the goal off a feed from Mike Renshaw. It was goalie Cooper, though, who actually proved the difference. In one 22-minute span, the Cosmos battered him with 11 shots, but none creased the net. Kyle's hot foot finally cooled in the championship game against the Philadelphia Atoms in Dallas. The Atoms controlled the game and captured the title with a 2–0 victory.

Wrote Kyle of the championship tilt: "The Atoms had been playing soccer for only eight months, but had put on a remarkable surge to make it to the finals. Playing without their two top scorers, they put on a display of determination and hustle befitting any champion. They took control of the game early and dominated play through the first twenty minutes. With nearly sixty-five minutes gone, Roy Evans and Mike Renshaw were chasing a loose ball down in the left wing corner. Renshaw was called for a foul and Evans was awarded a free kick. He drove it low across the 6-yard box to the far goal post. Defender John Best lunged for the ball with one leg. It glanced off his foot and caromed into the net just a few inches inside the uprights for the first score. We had scored on ourselves, and the Atoms led 1–0.

"With just 13 minutes remaining, we were moving the ball deep into Atom territory as Ilija Mitic and I were working a give-and-go. It ended in a shot from about eight yards out, but Atom goalie Bob Rigby sprang high and deflected the ball with his fingertips. It slammed against the crossbar and rebounded out front to Mohammed Attiah on the 18-yard line. Attiah's right-footed shot bounded toward the far post but Rigby lunged again and kicked it aside. With that reprieve the Atoms took control and scored the final goal with 4:15 to play."

For Kyle, the championship loss hardly dampened the overall success of his premier season. If the scoring title wasn't enough to soften the final defeat then copping the Rookie of the Year award certainly was. Said Newman of Kyle's remarkable season: "I would have never believed last spring that he would be the league's leading scorer. But his attitude was so good and he wanted to learn. In preseason, in all the scrimmage games, he kept on doing everything right. I'm delighted that he has been awarded this high honor."

Delighted too was Kyle's father. Kyle Sr., the former all-pro running back for the New York Giants, had never sought to influence his son to play football. In fact, his major admonition to Kyle Jr. had been to make sure that he prepared himself for something outside of athletics when his playing days were over. Says Kyle of his rapport with his father: "I sought his counsel and advice on what college to attend, whether to choose soccer over football, and many other things of lesser importance. He has always been a good counselor who helps me look at the situation objectively and then leaves the final decision to me. I know, too, that he is always there, and will continue to be, whenever I need him most." Nonetheless, Kyle Jr., from early age, realized that he would not be able to count on his well-known father to shape his life. "I am sure that his name has enhanced my image and opened a lot of doors for me. But one thing I am committed to, and that is making it alone without leaning on my father's name to get me through life. My name may be Kyle Rote, but I am still my own man. That's a lesson both my parents made sure I learned."

If Kyle's image needed any further enhancement after his rookie year, it got it when he competed in ABC-TV's

Superstars event in Florida. Says Kyle: "The inward challenge was three-fourths the fun of Superstars. I had set up certain objectives during my rookie season with the Tornado, and now this had given me something to shoot toward beyond those soccer goals. Since I felt no pressure to "win" the Superstars event, I enjoyed preparing myself to be in the best possible shape—whatever the outcome."

The finals competition called for participation in seven of ten events: sprinting, running, swimming, tennis, golfing, bowling, cycling, weight lifting, baseball hitting, and negotiation of an obstacle course. Kyle chose to stay out of the weight-lifting, running, and obstacle course events and worked his training program around the others. His confidence in his swimming ability took a quick dive the first day he jumped into the Dallas YMCA pool. Looking forward to a two-hundred-yard warmup, he found himself out of breath after only fifteen yards. For tennis, bowling, hitting golf balls, and baseballs, Kyle found a welcome at the Bronco Bowl, a sporting emporium where the balls come in all sizes.

Kyle's training program obviously helped. In *Beyond the Goal,* he describes the goings-on in Florida: "The first day of competition began early. It was still semi-dark and 32 degrees for the opening event, tennis. I was pitted against O. J. Simpson in the first match. Simpson jumped out to a 4–2 and 30–15 lead in the 1-set match. I then began to lob the ball to him, steadied my own shots, and came back to beat him, 6–4. I then came from behind again to beat John Havlicek, 6–3, and went on to take Jim McMillian, 6–4.

"Immediately after the tennis matches I rushed to the golf course where I competed with Dick Anderson, Peter Rose, Stan Smith, John Havlicek, Brin Oldfield and Franco Harris. We played nine holes and I shot a 43 to Anderson's 41, good enough for second place and seven points. These seven plus the ten for tennis gave me a total of seventeen.

"Later that day I picked up another 20 points by beating Bob Seagren by a stroke in the 100-meter swimming event

for first place (10 points) and bowling 214 for another first
and 10 more points. What a day! I was totally exhausted
but pleased that I had collected 37 points going into the
final day.

"Although I knew several of the participants personally,
there were many I did not know. Karl Schranz, a superb
skier from Austria, is reported to have said, 'I know all zese
guys except zis Juneeor, suppo-zed soccer fellow. Whoo ees
zis Rrowt Juneeor?' Many, of course, knew the name because of my dad. Mary Lynne tells the story of a little old
man who sat beside her during the events. He was having
the time of his life watching all the athletes. There was another man beside him and he was telling him what was
going on, except he really didn't know. He thought Arthur
Ashe was Reggie Jackson, Stan Smith was John Havlicek.
He didn't know one player from another, but he had names
for everybody; that is, until he came to me. Then he said,
'I don't know who *that* is.' His friend replied, 'Why, that's
Kyle Rote.' The little man stood up, leaned way over the
bleachers, and squinting down into the sun, looked; then
he sat back down and said, 'He certainly has held his age
well, hasn't he?'

"The second day I competed in the bicycle race, coming
in second and picking up another 7 points for a total of 44.
Ard Schenk and I were neck-and-neck in the bicycle race
when Jim McMillian tried to come around Anderson.
Their wheels touched, and the wing nut on McMillian's
front axle neatly sheared the spokes on Anderson's rear
wheel. McMillian fell, leaving quantities of his knee and
thigh on the track. Anderson limped along for awhile;
finally got off, threw his bike down in understandable dis-
gust and walked away.

"Surprisingly, I failed to score in the baseball hitting
which I had won in the semifinals. First place went to Stan
Smith, and in the half-mile run it was Bob Seagren, with
Dick Anderson very close.

"However, my 44 points were enough to edge out
Seagren who had a final total of 38. It was one of the

greatest days of my life. Along with the trophy, I received the Fram trophy for being the Superstar of the Year for 1974. I received a check for $54,500 (which represented my total earnings for all Superstar competition that year)— thirty-eight times more than I had made during the entire '73 soccer season. In addition, Mary Lynne and I had the joy of designating $5,000 of Fram's money for our favorite charity—the Special Olympics.

"Another goal had been met. Lynne and I had tithed ten percent or more of our income ever since we were married so we certainly didn't stop now. The Lord had been good to us and we wanted to share what we received. Winning Superstars 1974 was an inward challenge—one that began, and ended, with the prayer, 'Lord, help me to do my best whether I finish first or last.' "

The superstar victory did more, though, than enrich Kyle or his church. It gave pro soccer in the United States a new respectability. Here was an athlete "better" than stars from a number of other sports, not just someone who could kick a ball around. Here was a new superstar that kids could look up to and, as they did, they had to take notice of his sport. No longer would soccer players be relegated to second-class status among America's impressionable youth.

As the first American emissary for the game, however, Kyle may have paid a price that at the time was none too clear to him. Coach Newman explained: "I don't think any of us were surprised that he won. We all followed him closely and cheered him on. We were super-excited for him, but I don't think it did his game any good. The following year soccer improved and Kyle didn't improve his own game, because he was so much into the Superstars competition. And whereas I think he's done great for the game, as winning Superstars and getting the NASL and whatever into the forefront, he hasn't done himself a lot of good. I think he'd have been better if he hadn't been so well-known. He'd have been a better player. But he's had to live up to a standard and it's been a lot of pressure for him.

Everybody wants to see him and often they're disappointed in his ability. It's unfair to him."

Kyle, for the most part, concurs: "As a person, I don't think winning Superstars has changed my life. I hope that it hasn't changed my attitude on life or my outlook on life, just in the opportunities. I've had to travel and meet people and in business opportunities and that type of thing. Soccer-wise, Superstars has been very good because now in many cities whenever I do a clinic we get a much bigger turnout than we might have gotten. The national television coverage helped in relation to other sports because here's a soccer player beating a football player, beating a basketball player, beating a baseball player. It must mean that soccer is not just a catchall sport for mediocre athletes.

"But in a personal way it put more pressure on me, because I'd go into a city, for example, and people who had seen me on Superstars would read pre-game writeups in the newspapers and would come and see the game expecting to see more than they were going to see."

Kyle went on to win two more of the annual Superstar competitions, made hundreds of thousands of dollars from the victories and the resultant business deals but still managed to keep his sense of balance. Both Newman and Al Miller, who took over the Tornado coaching job before the '76 season began, agree that Kyle has handled fame well. Says Miller: "If you ever want somebody to have superstar status, you want somebody like Kyle because he's such a great representative, he's so good with kids, he's got so much patience with people, so much understanding. His whole attitude about sports is so right. I haven't seen any kind of change in him. He's got a tremendous respect factor on the club. Everybody understands what he has to go through. He's mobbed by kids and people every place we go. We have to get his phone disconnected at hotels because he won't get his rest if we don't. Everytime we go to a town, television, radio, newspapers all want to see him. He's just got a big schedule compared to all the rest of the people and I think our players understand that and respect him for it because he's so level-headed about it. I think he has everything in pretty good perspective. One of the first things that he and I worked on when I first came here was his conflicts of interest. I don't feel that in any way, shape, or form any of his appearances or engagements hurt him. I don't feel that at all."

Adds Newman: "He never expected special treatment after the first Superstars win. He was very, very careful about getting into the position of asking for any special treatment, of asking for anything more. You couldn't fault the lad. He knew how to handle that type of situation. There are many players who couldn't do it. I shudder to think what it could have done to some of the other players I had. Kyle could do it very well. He's a very mature lad, very mature. He knew exactly how far he could go and what he should do and so on."

While Kyle regularly tithed and gave money to charities, Newman was a little perturbed that he did not choose to spend his winnings in another way. Says the coach: "He's a very frugal man. I don't think he's supergenerous. I mean he won the Superstars competition but I don't remember him ever getting hold of all the players and taking them out to a boozer or out to dinner or anything like that. Everybody knew he'd won thousands of dollars. In fact, I know he made probably $100,000 the first year (after the Superstars victory), but the players, who were his buddies, who really put him there, never saw any of it, which was a bit disappointing for Kyle. But I don't think the players resented it very much. Only one or two ever bothered about it. The sensible ones realized that he had something to offer the game and it wasn't his ability, that wasn't going to do it. The name he'd made would bring the crowds in."

Attracting bigger crowds and making more personal appearances and coping with extra pressure may have hurt his game, but there were also other factors that contributed to the fact that Kyle scored only nine points in the '76 season and played in only eighteen games, seven of which he did not start. Says Miller: "The problem, if there is a problem with Kyle, is his lack of experience. There's a saying, 'What Lenny doesn't learn, big Len will never do.' I think Kyle is somewhat of an example of this in that he did not have the good background as a young player that he should have had to be a great professional. I think that had he started playing soccer as a young boy and maybe built his ground floor correctly, he'd be a supertalent at this point.

"I think he's done a tremendous amount, more than the average person could do, having had such a late start. So I think that when I rate Kyle, Kyle has got superstar status because he's really the first American soccer player to ever be talked about. He got off to a great start. He had a lot of things on his side. He had a very famous father, he won the Superstars, which put him in another category of publicity, and his agents have done a super job in getting him out in the public and promoting him and so forth. A lot of people look at him as another Pele, as the American Pele, and I think that's unfair for Kyle because, while he's a professional, he's not the superstar Pele is."

Newman is more precise in detailing some of Kyle's weaknesses: "I don't think he sees the game quick enough. His ability to control the ball and change direction quickly is not good. His ability to beat a man was nonexistent. He could never fake a man very well. He was never comfortable with the ball at his feet. Those were his biggest weaknesses. Another weakness was that he wasn't . . . well, if I say he wasn't brave enough, that can be misconstrued because I certainly don't think he was a coward. But he's a big lad and he should be able to intimidate defenders, make them look out of the corner of their eyes for him. But he didn't, he was too good. We asked him and we begged him and we instructed him to go and mix it up in there, force people into making mistakes, because that was what he could do. He could run, he was strong and so to use that we said any time the ball's in the box, go after it, make people make mistakes, but he wouldn't.

"We didn't want him to be dirty, but if he could get to

the ball at the same time as the goalkeeper, we wanted him to hit the goalie, as long as it was reasonably fair. We didn't want him to get sent off for something. But we could never get him to make contact with people and that was a big weakness of his. I think he could have improved his game quite a lot if he'd have done that."

Kyle believes that the toughest problem he had at first was developing his mental quickness while in a game situation. Says he: "In college you pretty much have time to receive the ball, trap it, look up, see where your opponent is and then make the decision. In professional soccer, I found it a lot like baseball. When I played outfield, before every pitch I asked myself, 'If the ball's hit to me right now on the ground, what am I going to do with it? If it's in the air, what am I going to do?' That was just a little game to keep me concentrating. In soccer it was pretty much the same thing. I had to begin to think, because we had some Brazilians on the team at that time and they could hit the ball 50 or 60 yards without even looking at you. So I had to ask myself the same questions. If they hit me the ball right now, what am I going to do? I had to learn to have my mind almost made up before the ball even came so that I could play a lot of one-touch soccer, which is what Ron wanted."

But Coach Newman had another problem. He asserts that he sometimes played Kyle when he really did not want to, and that some other players on the squad resented it. Says Newman: "There were some who resented the fact and he did play sometimes because of who he was. It was difficult to leave him out of the side because so much promotion had been done because of him. I used to have pro-Rote and anti-Rote fans. I used to get letters saying 'Why don't you play Rote?' and the same day, 'What the hell did you play Rote again for?' Nobody could agree. The people that probably knew the game better didn't want Kyle. Those who were pro-All-American boy felt that he should play regardless of what happened. At that time (1972–73), when I played him I was doing it for the sake of soccer, but soccer has gotten to be such a cutthroat business now that I don't think it could be done. You have to win, otherwise you have no job. In those days soccer seemed to be the biggest thing, you had to win for soccer."

Notwithstanding the position he was in, vis-à-vis Kyle, Newman says they "always got on well. We were of a different mould and we clashed at times, but I think we respected each other. I always respected him. I thought he was very personable and outgoing and everybody liked him. He didn't mix too well with the lads because he wasn't the sort of bread-and-butter player most of the lads are that come into the game. They've come up the hard way and it's been tough for them. He sort of inherited a lot of what he got."

Although Kyle agrees that his name did help a bit, he doesn't think it caused any trouble with his teammates. "I've been treated more than fairly," he says. "We have different interests. For example, a lot of our guys, and it's a tradition in England, go and grab a beer after practice. That was never part of my upbringing and it's not part of my relationship with my wife. It's part of the culture in England, so wives understand. My wife would never understand and I would not want to make her try to understand that, because I enjoy coming home and just kind of collapsing. As far as off-the-field activity, we do a lot of things together like tennis or parties and that kind of thing, but we each have retained our individual differences."

Kyle also had to adjust to the individual differences of Newman and Miller. When the latter took over in '76, Kyle had come off back-to-back 16-point seasons and needed some boosting. Instead, Miller's plan for the team was such that Kyle's playing time and game suffered even more. Says Miller: "My decision when I came to the Tornados was that everybody had a target player and I was going to play without one. I looked for the skillful player and I got this boy, Jeff Bourne, who just did a super job for us. In essence, he beat Kyle out for his job. He could contribute more."

Being benched is no easy thing for any professional athlete, but Kyle took his change in playing status in characteristically good form. Says he: "I don't think I resent or regret anything that's happened to me, which shows you that I probably don't have a realistic view. But I mean that, I really believe that out of everything that happens to you, you can find something positive. So for me it may have been a good time to get my head straight—ego-wise. I'm not saying it wasn't, but that it was a good time for me certainly to see a new style of play that I wasn't familiar with and to learn a lot from Jeff who replaced me."

According to Miller, Kyle's reaction was a measure of the young man's character. Said the coach at the time: "I don't think any athlete likes to sit, but he hasn't become nasty about it. I think this is why I like Kyle so much. Instead of complaining and asking to be traded or anything else, he's just looked the problem straight in the eye and he's working like hell to see if he can lick the problem and win his job back."

After Kyle's 9-point '76 season, Miller still had faith in Kyle's ability to bounce back. Said Miller: "He's easy to coach. He comes to team meetings and takes notes. That should tell you a little about him. We have a program going with him to refine his skills. I think once he gets those, he can be very effective as a striker. He does have something to contribute. He's a very bright person and he's been so dedicated, he somehow makes things happen to you when he gets his chance." At the start of the '77 season, Kyle's status was basically unchanged. "We couldn't find a way to use him," Miller said. But then the coach began teaming Kyle on the front line with veteran English First Division forwards Alan Hinton and John O'Hare. O'Hare worked as a ball-control specialist, while Hinton, an excellent passer, often crossed the ball high to Kyle's head. "John and Alan have really helped Kyle," said Tornado goalkeeper Kenny Cooper. "John takes a lot of pressure off him."

For sure, something seemed to be going better for Kyle. Early in May, he scored the only goal in a 1–0 win over the Los Angeles Aztecs. Of the next half dozen games, Dallas took only two, and in one of them, at Toronto, Kyle scored two goals. When the team returned to Dallas for a June 11 game against Team Hawaii, he continued his scoring streak with the first hat trick of his career. "To me, Kyle is really beginning to find himself," said Hinton. "He's improved greatly and I think he'll continue to improve. He's proved to himself and to the fans that he can deliver the goods."

Through the first two-thirds of the season Kyle did just that, scoring ten goals and three assists. Four of the goals proved to be game-winners and he became the highest scorer and total point maker of any Tornado player. Perhaps his most significant advance, however, came when Miller used him, for the first time, as one of five Dallas shooters in a tie-breaker at Seattle. "It is, I'm sure, a good sign," said Kyle. And so were his final stats for the year: eleven goals, six assists for 28 points. That output was good enough to land him in tenth place among the league's scoring leaders. But, in typical fashion, Kyle would not let his outstanding comeback from a few mediocre seasons get out of proportion. Said he: "I don't view my self-worth by how I do as a soccer player. I'm not a soccer player who just happens to be in Dallas right now. I'm a human being who happens to be playing soccer for a living."

And living a good, family-oriented, spiritually based life is basically what Kyle has in mind for the future. "I have to assume that I won't play more than today," says Kyle. "What I've been doing is developing the financial security which will allow me to take two years off to finish my schooling once my career ends. I definitely want to finish my work in the seminary (at Southern Methodist University). A few years ago, I said I wanted to be a minister. Now I'm more interested in becoming a Christian businessman, or by definition, a lay minister. Mary Lynne and I both want to be good stewards." Still, before the '77 season Kyle said that he would like to play soccer for "at least another four, possibly five, years." If that's the case, there is little question that superstar Kyle Rote will become a fully recognized soccer star.

DEREK SMETHURST

He's called the Stork and he makes deliveries almost every day he's working. Tampa Bay's leading obstetrician? No, this stork delivers goals for the Rowdies. And all he has to do with babies is make opposition defenders and goalkeepers cry like them. At 6 ft. 1 in., and weighing in at 165 lbs. (before games), the Stork certainly fits the billing. His ankles are so thin, socks have yet to be found that will stay up. He fills out his uniform just about as well as those fashion models do in "le Sack."

How then has this stringbean managed to become one of the most prolific scorers in the NASL? It's obviously a case of mind over matter for the 30-year-old forward who has scored 57 goals in three NASL seasons. Says Derek: "I think everyone can be a super athlete if he has the basic talent to begin with. But the guy who really wants to achieve prepares himself mentally. Like in the 100-yard dash, the sprinter runs his race every day in his head. Over and over. He runs that race until he can actually see himself winning. I concentrate on my role as a goal scorer until I can actually see myself scoring the goal. Until I actually see exactly what I must do to score. But knowing what to do is only half the battle. Once you know what to do, you must go out and do it."

For Derek that means out-foxing and out-running the considerably larger—and slower—fullbacks in the league. He does it much the same way former New York Knick

forward Bill Bradley used to get open for shots at the hoop:
by running without the ball. Says Derek: "Defenders don't
like to run after you. When forwards start running them,
they don't know how to cope. Their mental attitude goes
right down the drain, it disappears and they go looking for
someone to kick." He also can be cagey about it. "I really
try to hide behind defenders where they can't see me. You
have to move diagonally across the field, then sort of turn
around, throw your weight one way, while going the other
toward where the ball's coming. That's the only way to get
away from your man."

At times, Derek will even have the audacity to, well,
muscle his marker out of the way. He even thinks he has
physically had the better of his defenders. "I feel that I've
hit the big defenders in this game a damn sight harder than
they have hit me. People laugh about it and wonder how I
did it." The element of surprise is, no doubt, a key to it.
When defenders are chasing a shadow around all day and
suddenly *it* finds them, the contact can be pretty crushing.

Of course, there is also Derek's pure speed that helps.
"You burn up a tremendous amount of energy in the goal
mouth, where it's crowded, where you have to beat bigger
players head-to-head. To beat them to a position, I must
rely on my speed. And when I beat them, they're not so big
anymore, are they?"

Derek's career of cutting defenders down to size began in
his native South Africa where he played for Durbin City
for three years. At age 20, he was snatched up by the English First Division team, Chelsea, and stayed through five
difficult seasons. The problem was that he mostly played as
a reserve for Peter Osgood, "one of the best center forwards in the world at that time," according to Derek, and
at midfield. "It was so mentally hard on me to wait for my
chance, especially when you know you can play on a regular basis. I had to get out of there."

And that he did in 1972. He gambled with Second
Division Millwell—and lost. "Millwell looked like it was
going to move to the First Division, but it didn't. As it

turned out, that was the worst move I ever made. The place was a dump. There was a terrible atmosphere there for soccer. For 18 months, I played on and off. I was injured. I recovered. I was injured again. I recovered again. It got to be a little too much to take. I couldn't get any adequate medical treatment. The physical therapy expert's idea for my ills was to take two aspirins and go to bed.

"The greatest injury was to myself. I could have played my way back to Division One. I didn't. I had a negative attitude. I didn't play the way I was capable of playing. I was so disenchanted I was seriously considering retirement."

And Millwell wouldn't sell Derek to another English club. The management asked for 30,000 pounds (about $70,000) for Derek, deliberately pricing him out of the English market. "No one would pay that kind of money for me. Who wanted an injured player?"

Eddie Firmani, that's who. The Rowdies' coach had seen Derek play at Chelsea in 1972 and remembered the speed, the moves, the goals. When Millwell coach Gordon Jago let Tampa Bay know that Smethurst was available, Firmani placed an overseas call. Recalls Derek: "It took me about one minute and one-half to make up my mind. I didn't even ask about salary. I didn't care. They told me to come on over and make it a holiday to see if I'd like it. My legs hurt like the devil and I needed the rest."

In April 1975, Derek and wife Nina made the trip and liked what they saw. The climate was especially pleasing. At Chelsea Derek often had to contend with rotten field conditions. Said he: "There's too much mud on the grounds in England, and the ball just sticks in the middle of the field. The weather really does make a big difference over here. The mud took a lot of me. I pulled muscles in my thigh three times in England running up the middle. We played on hard ground in South Africa, and that was good. It was easy to run with the ball."

The 1975 season was near-perfect for Derek from beginning to end: a goal in his first game and an NASL championship. With 18 goals and 3 assists, he fell just 10 points short of Steve David for the scoring title. One record he did establish: eight consecutive games scoring a goal. Said Derek: "When I came over here, it was like a breath of fresh air. A new country, new soccer ball, new players around you, players who create chances for you." But he obviously still had his old magic. "Everyone's got a knack for doing something. I've just got a knack for being there and knocking the ball in. Ninety per cent of your goals come from other people setting you up, and the rest come from mistakes by defenders."

Before the next season began, Derek signed a four-year pact with the Rowdies. He and his wife began building a four-bedroom house. He was a happy player. It showed. His greatest game in American soccer came in New York in June. Before 42,611 fans and another six million or so watching the nationally televised game, Derek scored a hat trick in the Rowdies' 5–1 victory. What made it more enjoyable was the post-game TV interview. "That was nice going on television. I like to do TV commercials and commentating. And that was the first time I'd ever been on national TV."

But what made Derek's day truly special were Pele's comments about him: "That number twelve. He not make three goals with his feet. He not make three goals because he was in free zone. He use his mind." Derek, an easygoing, modest man, was genuinely flattered. "Pushing those three goals in against New York and the compliment from Pele was my finest moment. Pele is the *king,* no doubt. To have the king say such a thing about you is very gratifying. To have him praise you for your mental powers is something else, when his are so great."

Derek had another hat trick game during the season and exploded for four goals in a 7–0 romp over the Connecticut Bicentennials, but his most spectacular single goal of the year came against the Philadelphia Atoms. The game was tied 1–1 in overtime when Derek, his back to the goal, received a pass from Clyde Best 25 yards out. Suddenly he whirled around and blasted the ball into the right corner of the net. The goalkeeper never saw it.

"My ultimate goal," says Derek, "is to play every game as well as I can. To use my mind, as well as my body, to score goals. That's what I'm paid for. That's what I am. A goal scorer." And as for those puffing defenders, any tips so that they can keep getting paid? "All they have to do is look behind them. That's where I'll be," says Derek with a smile, "most of the time."

MIKE STOJANOVIC

For vitually all other players in the NASL, the kind of season that Mike Stojanovic (stoy-yon-vich) had in 1977 would have been just dandy, but it had to be a little disappointing for the Rochester Lancers' star striker. His fifth place finish in the league scoring race (behind David, Smethurst, Best, and Chinaglia) on fourteen goals and five assists—thirty-three points—was not exactly what "the gunner," as he is called in Rochester, had in mind at the outset of the campaign. "This is my season," he had said before the season's opening whistle. "I'm certainly going to make a run for the scoring title. I did a good job last year, but that was with players who really didn't know each other until the second half of the season. Knowing the players from the start will definitely be a benefit."

Perhaps the idea was right but, in fact, the Yugoslavian-born Stojanovic scored three more goals and two more assists in 1976, his first year in the league, in the same number of games (twenty-four). Whatever his expectations or statistics, Mike is unquestionably one of the most dangerous forwards in the game. His excellence was recognized when he was named to the league's second team all-star squad.

Before he joined the Lancers, Mike proved it by being one of Yugoslavia's top goal getters for thirteen years. One of his favorite goals came in 1969 when his struggling Radhicki Kraguden team needed to win six of its last seven games to avoid being demoted to the country's Second Division. Recalls Mike: "I scored the winning goal to keep my team in the First Division. It was an exciting moment. It would have looked bad if we were dropped. I played very well the last seven games. I scored only seven goals that season, but five were in those games. I'm proud of that."

Mike could also be proud of his first two years' performance in North America. Playing for the Toronto White Eagles of the National Soccer League of Canada, he established a league record in 1974 by scoring fifty-four goals in thirty-six games. The next year in Toronto, he slipped a bit, but managed to net forty-two goals, good enough to take the league's scoring crown again.

When the White Eagles' coach Dragan (Don) Popovic was hired by the Lancers, he brought Mike along with him. Says Popovic: "Mike is a special kind of player. He has a fast start, can score and can cross the ball beautifully. He has a tremendous right foot, a fantastic smell for the goal. Every midfielder enjoys a player like him. A midfielder can loft the ball behind the defense and know that a Stojanovic-type player is fast enough to reach the ball." Mike rates himself, teammate Ibraim Silva, the Aztecs' Steve David, and the Rowdies' Steve Wegerle as the fastest players in the league.

Mike also doesn't hesitate to rank himself as one of the best players around. "I'm a maestro, a European trickster," he told the press early in his first season with the Lancers. His braggadocio carries over onto the field where, some say, he's a genuine ball hog.

Among his teammates there are mixed feelings about Mike's cocky attitude. Lancer goalkeeper Blagoje Tamindic, a friend of Mike's since their playing days in Canada says, "He is something special. He has an opinion about everything. He tries to be perfect. That's good for a sportsman. He hollers at people on the field, not because they've made a mistake, but because he wants the ball. If he scores five, he cries that he needs six. If someone doesn't understand him, they can take him the wrong way. That's the way he is. He has everything a forward needs. If you leave him alone with one guy, it's a 70-30 chance it's a goal." Mike Bakic, another White Eagle whom the Lancers acquired for the '77 season, agrees: "I don't think we've been using him enough. Even when Stojanovic is double-covered we should give him the ball because with his speed he still has a chance to score."

Nonetheless, others on the squad believe Mike plays too much for himself. Said forward Silva: "If Stojanovic played for the team, we'd score more and he'd score more. He knows what he should do, but sometimes he forgets."

To Silva's remarks, Mike responded, "No, no, no," and defended his play. "I'm a striker; I have to keep the ball. I'm the man they pay to score. I shouldn't have to watch my teammates and give them the ball when they want it. They should watch me and give me the ball when I want it. They haven't been doing that this season ['77]. I get the ball, but always two or three seconds too late. They pass to me when I'm covered and not when I'm open."

Mike's problems with teammates may have had something to do with the threat he made to quit after the '77 season was over. But he also blamed his physical condition, the press, and the Lancers' fans. Said Mike: "I'm tired. Every game I play injured. My back is bad. My foot is bad. My face is sore from being elbowed so many times. In my mind I have to stop it. I've been angry with the press because I think the writers are against me. Things haven't been going as well for me this year as last and some of them have been too harsh in their criticism. The spectators have really been giving me trouble, too. They're riding me because of my style of play. They don't understand me. I'm not Yugoslavian. I'm not Canadian. I am a Rochester Lancer."

Coach Popovic thought he knew what was truly ailing Mike. He attributed his star's desire to quit, to the fact that his wife Rosa and infant daughter, Vera, were still in Toronto. Although Mike saw them about twice a week, the strain was great on the family. Said Popovic, "If we bring his family here next year I think he'll change his mind. I don't believe he's going to quit." Popovic was right. "The Gunner" remains a Rochester Lancer. And fans throughout the continent can be thankful for that.

AL TROST

Watch out Steve Garvey, you might have some competition as the favorite Mr. Nice Guy athlete in the Los Angeles area. Though he might not get a junior high school named after him, as the Dodger first baseman did, Al Trost of the newly created California Surf is sure to impress locals with his boyish good looks, friendly disposition, and exemplary manners. But what should make the fans even happier about the new gangly, 6 foot, 2 inch All-American boy on the block is that he just happens to be, according to most observers of NASL soccer, the best home-grown player in the America. Curiously, he plays midfield, where a foreign passport is practically required in the league.

Not too surprisingly, Al is a product of the St. Louis soccer scene. To give some indication of the importance of St. Louis as a breeding ground for American NASL players, it is estimated that more than half of the Americans in the league hail from the City of the Arch. On the St. Louis Stars all but four of Al's teammates were born and raised in that city. Like many of the better soccer players in the area, Al went to St. Louis University, the collegiate soccer power in the country. Of the last eighteen National Collegiate Athletic Association championships since 1959, ten have been won by SLU.

Before he got to the soccer college, Al already had quite a career going locally. Raised in North St. Louis, the youngest of five brothers and sisters, Al began kicking a ball around when he was six, that is, when he wasn't acting as ball boy for his older brothers' teams. In his soccer-oriented family, brother Tom, thirteen years Al's senior, was All-American at St. Louis University, and Al's father coached in the Catholic Youth Council program. Maybe most helpful was brother Wally who, though he and his soccer friends were six years older than Al, let him play in their games. Says Al: "Playing with kids so much older than I was really helped me develop my game."

Al gave up his other sports—baseball and basketball—by the time he was thirteen and played only soccer, mostly for his parish teams. Management must have been effective, since Al set his sights on entering the priesthood and entered St. Louis Prep Seminary South. Although he was known as a good player, no college recruiters bothered to watch him, what with clergyhood beckoning him.

Then, before graduating, Al changed his mind. Recalls Al: "It was a most difficult time. One of the most important decisions I've ever made. The reasons? Well, personal reasons, really."

Soon word was out and SLU coach Bob Guelker came by to see Al play and quickly persuaded him to go with the Billikens. By the time Al was playing varsity ball in 1968—his sophomore year—Guelker had departed and the team was in the hands of Harry Keough. Keough has been there since and he still ranks Al as one of the very best he has ever had. Says Keough: "He had this ability when the ball looked like it was out of control, to stick out his leg, and get it back. He could beat so many opponents that way. And he came up with the big play so often for us, scoring the crucial goal, real inspirational stuff. And he had the speed to pass anyone. And he's the nicest person you'd ever want to meet."

Al's college soccer record was about as good as it could be. While SLU lost in the 1968 NCAA quarterfinals to Maryland, it took the national crown the next two years, and Al, beyond a doubt, was the team's most valuable player. In both championship years, moreover, he copped

the Hermann Trophy as the college player of the year. Recalling those golden seasons, Al says: "I guess my junior
year was a thrill, winning the championship, but we were
the favorites [over San Francisco] then. The senior year
was bigger, really, we only had three seniors as starters.
There were the rivalries, too, the games against SIU
(Southern Illinois) and Quincy. Especially playing at Quincy, it's a small place, and soccer was all they had . . . they
all used to turn out, it was like playing in a snakepit. We
knew those games were always going to be hard, brutal
games."

Al planned to go to law school after graduation in 1971,
but decided to go into teaching instead. Before pursuing
that fully, however, he devoted himself to getting prepared
for the Olympics, a year away in Munich. He became a
member of the U.S. team in the 1971 Pan-American Games
and virtually the same squad went on to the Olympics.
There, it became the first American team ever to make it
through the qualifying rounds into the finals. Al's Olympic
coach, Bob Guelker, believed that to do its best, the U.S.
had to concentrate on defense. The strategy worked well
until the final round in Munich, when the U.S. tied Moroc-
co, 0–0, then lost 0–3 to Malaysia, and 0–7 to West Germany. The closest the U.S. came to scoring in the last game
was a shot by Al that hit the post.

Al came away from that shellacking impressed. Said he:
"It opened my eyes to what soccer really was. The difference between the West Germans and us was just amazing. I'd never seen the game played on such a high level,
and so fast. It seemed their players were infallible. As an
American player, you know, I'd won NCAA titles, I'd been
college player of the year, I was on the Olympic team, how
much further could I go? Then I see these players, and I was
amazed at how far behind I was. No, it wasn't discourag-
ing. Just the opposite. I started to think, 'Hey, what can I
do to catch up? I've missed something.' I wanted to come
home and tell everyone, 'Hey, you won't believe this, but
we're so far behind, let's get going.' I felt we needed to

broaden our game, speed it up."

When Al began his pro career the next spring for the Stars, the Olympic experience proved most valuable. Said Al: "I found pro ball not as much as it was made out to be. Participating in the Olympics, I'd seen the game played at that level. I wasn't surprised at all because I was familiar with a higher level of play." Al adds that the NASL style "is the roughest, hardest, and fastest game that I have ever experienced. Players coming out of college think that they are going to glide right into the professional ranks and that they will be able to compete on that level of play compared to what they see and experience on the college level. I can only say that they will learn very quickly that it's going to be a lot harder than they anticipate."

Al's pro career got off to the kind of start that was right in step with his earlier triumphs. In St. Louis' first home game of '73, Al was on the bench when midfielder Larry Hausmann suffered a separated shoulder. Al went in and has never returned to the bench. Says Al: "I was a young, confident St. Louisand, and I felt I could compete in the NASL, that I could do well. They were just beginning to bring better foreign players into the league and I looked at them and I felt I wasn't that far behind them. It was mainly that they had more experience than I did. The biggest adjustment for me was in becoming a more disciplined player, especially in training."

Al may have been lucky that so many of his teammates were also from St. Louis. At least all of them had played pretty much the same kind of soccer. In *The Simplest Game,* soccer writer Paul Gardner calls it "the nearest we have to an indigenous American style. St. Louis soccer is best characterized as an 'off the ball' style: it involves a good deal of movement and running by players who are not in possession of the ball. The progress of the ball itself is accomplished mainly by first-time passing, and it is rare to see a St. Louis player dwelling on the ball or engaging in a protracted dribble. (Indeed, it sometimes looks as though St. Louis players regard the ball as a noxious object to be got rid of as soon as possible.)"

Basically then, St. Louis soccer is played with short passes, and it is this aspect of the style that Star coach John Sewell attempted to alter with the Stars. Sewell preferred that the Stars rely more on the "flighted ball," or longer passes. Al readily admits that "I have not been accustomed throughout my development here in St. Louis to this style of play. I have, over the past couple years, had a better understanding of how Sewell wants us to play and perform on the field."

And Sewell has been largely satisfied with Al's development. Says he: "Al is still on the way up. He is becoming one of the premier midfielders in the league. It's the goal he's after. He'll go forward trying to work an opening for himself or someone else. He makes good use of the ball, he reads the game well. The negative aspects of his play are his defensive abilities—tackling, picking up opponents. Al is a good listener, he works hard, he's getting better all the time."

Al agrees with Sewell's assessment: "I'm not a good tackler, I think it's my body structure, my center of gravity is high, my legs are thin and real long." He also adds a bit of criticism that Sewell failed to mention: "I think, for my height, I ought to win more balls in the air. I try to put that right by practicing with pendulum balls."

How would Al assess his strengths? Says he: "I don't have the great individual skills that some midfielders have. I get over that by having a better knowledge of where the players are, where they are around me. I use players around me well." Al gives his teammates much credit for his success: "No one carries a team, it's a group effort. I've been fortunate enough to be at the right place to score. Not enough credit though, goes to those who started the offense, worked the ball upfield and fed me the ball. More people should appreciate the action prior to the goal."

Al also stresses teamwork on the team that he coaches. In St. Louis, most of the players had to hold other jobs—the Stars were essentially a semipro team—and Al taught and coached at McLuer North High School. In 1975 he guided his team to their first state championship. Says Al: "It was one of the biggest thrills of my life. It gives you a great sense of accomplishment to work with a group of athletes and see them improve all the way to the title." There are, of course, frustrations in coaching for Al: "Sometimes I get a talented player who doesn't feel that he has to practice much. I can't stand complacency in a player; it drives me up the wall. I'll take that player and work his butt off to show him he's not as good as he thinks he is."

Al never had that problem himself. In his first year as a pro, he was named to the NASL All-Star team as an honorable mention. But a bigger thrill for him that year, 1973, came in an exhibition game against the Polish national team that had won the gold medal at Munich.

Played in New Britain, Connecticut, the match turned out to be one of those rare moments of glory for United States soccer. The Americans won, 1–0, and Al scored the goal. "I'd never shot a ball like that in my life. The ball came over from the left to Gene Geimer who had his back to the Polish goal, and he nodded it down for me. I ran on to it, near the corner of the area, and hit it first time, on the half-volley. No placement whatever, I just hit it. But it took off, and I felt immediately that it had a chance, that the goalkeeper wasn't going to get it. It must have been about a 20-yard shot, and it went high, just inside the near post. Then we held on for 20 minutes or so. It was a narrow field, so it was perfect for our defensive team. We made it, and after the game there were fans all over the field, they came up and talked, congratulating me on the goal. They were really nice to me, especially as most of them had come to see Poland. I guess they were impressed that we beat them."

Al continued to play for the national team over the next two years, although his teaching prevented him from regularly participating. In 1976, the new U.S. Coach, Walt Chyzowich, appointed him captain of the squad, a move that surprised John Sewell: "Al is a quiet player on the field. I feel he prefers to be led, rather than to lead."

Nonetheless, the team did well under Trost in the World Cup qualifying games against Mexico and Canada, though it just missed going on to the finals. With the U.S. and Canada having finished tied on points and with the same goal difference, a playoff was held in Port-au-Prince, Haiti, in December. In previous games the U.S. had tied the Canadians in Vancouver and between them 2–0 in Seattle, but the decisive game, a bitterly contested match, went to Canada, 3–0. The result, however, did not leave Al discouraged about the future promise of the national team: "In terms of development Americans have made in the last four or five years, we are on the right track now. I think from our experience on the tour we are competitive in the region in which we compete and against South America in terms of their style of play. I think we are going to improve drastically in the next four years and feel that they aren't going to improve that much. They are having problems now getting out of their old systems and styles of play and trying to modernize their game a lot more. But South Americans are more skilled than we are because that's their style. The climate is warmer so they play a slower game and do tricks with the ball."

With the demise of the St. Louis Stars, Al should have to perform less magic of his own. Wanting to give his wife Elna and two-year-old son Timothy more of his attention, turning full-time pro will help. Moreover, Al says, "It would give me the time to do a lot of things I've wanted to do for a long time. Like getting a coaching badge and my Masters. I'm working on it now, very slowly. And I'd like to get certification so that I can teach Phys. Ed. And I'd certainly reconsider retiring from the national team." Whatever Al does, he no doubt will do it well.

GEORGE BEST

"I think I've found a genius." The scouting report could not have been simpler. In the Protestant section of Belfast, Northern Ireland, 15-year-old George Best quickly caught the eye and captured the imagination of Manchester United's talent sleuth. The English First Division team was on a youth-building program in 1961, and little George, all 100 pounds of him, would be the perfect cornerstone for it. Courageous beyond his size, extraordinarily skillful with his feet, and possessed with an instinctive sense for the game, George had but one destiny: to rank among the few best forwards in soccer history.

Before George could claim entry to that group, however, he had to overcome one minor problem. When he and another young lad reported to Manchester, Mrs. Mary Fullaway, a club "mum," had twin beds ready for them; however, within 24 hours both lads were headed home. George always insisted that it was his mate who was homesick, which amused Mrs. Fullaway. Shy George soon returned when his father convinced him that there was nothing too bad about the big-city atmosphere of Manchester.

Within two years, George made his debut at Old Trafford, the home of United. Playing right wing, George was marked by Stuart Williams, a Welsh international fullback of considerable proportions. In a sensational performance, George teased and taunted and finally humiliated Williams with audacious ball control. The immediate response of

soccer writers and watchers was that a "second Stanley
Matthews" had come. It was not long before the comparison to the shuffling dazzler of the '30s and '40s had to
be abandoned. Unlike Sir Stanley, George relished the in-
fighting of the game and almost recklessly used sliding
tackles to take the ball away from opponents.

By the time George was 18, he was a world class player.
He became a Northern Ireland international, went on to
take two English Footballer of the Year awards and a European Footballer of the Year prize. While he was with
United, they won the English League Championship twice,
the Football Association Cup, and the European Cup.

With his huge success came fame so great that long-
haired, mod George was staggered. Young girls flocked to
his house, waited to catch a glimpse of him when he visited
one of the clothing boutiques he owned, tried to touch him
after games when he walked off the pitch. They screamed
with all the adolescent soul they could muster, as they did
for their other idols of the era, the Beatles. "It was really
overwhelming at first," George admitted, "and not a little
embarrassing. Mind you, I loved it. Who wouldn't. Everyone loves to be loved. I lapped it up. The more they
screamed for me, the more I would play up to it."

In the late '60s, living was easy for George, probably too
easy. An agent, a secretary, and a Jaguar served him well.
So, he thought, did liquor, which he drank with abandon,
and ingratiating "birds," whom he loved and abandoned.
Still, conflict ruled. A Gemini (born May 22, 1946), George
was two people. He yearned to drink; he regretted it afterwards. He flitted from girl to girl; he sought repose. He
could be as charming as a child; he brushed his way
through crowds of children without a moment's pause.

George could also make trouble. In 1970, he was suspended twenty-eight days and fined one hundred pounds
for knocking the ball out of the referee's hands after a
League Cup semifinal match in which he had been booked.
A year later, he drew a six-month suspension for having
received three bookings in twelve months. After disappear-

ing to London, Manchester United suspended him for two weeks. In 1972, he missed training and was fined two weeks wages and was forced to leave home and move into team lodgings. United finally gave up on George. After he was charged with assaulting a young woman in a Manchester nightclub, he was banned from such clubs, after which he skipped training and turned up in London.

George's explanation for this outlandish behavior is twofold: the English attitude toward athletes and his own sharp temper. Said George: "In England a professional athlete is tightly bound to a social system set up by the fans. They want their heroes to be sober, clean-cut, family men, and it just so happens that my lifestyle doesn't follow along those lines." As for his temper, George said at the time of his problems: "I hate myself for it, but I don't seem to be able to help it. It just proves that I am still young and that I still have a lot to learn."

Despite his disciplinary troubles, George's play at Manchester United, and in international matches, thrust him into the position of being one of the most valued soccer players. In 1972, the *Daily Mail* surveyed leading soccer managers around the world to have them assess George's style and worth. At the time, the record transfer fee was the 440,000 pounds (roughly $880,000 then) paid for Italian superstar Pietro Anastasi in 1968. Some of the experts refused to assess any monetary value. Said Hungarian Ferenc Puskas, "How can you price genius? I rate players as human beings and let the clubs assess their value in terms of money." Other replies:

Helenio Herrera, manager of Roma: "Together with Sandro Mazzola, I rate Best as number one in the world today. Both men are unsurpassed. Best's knowledge of the game is quite extraordinary, profound. His feeling for football is uncanny. But it is not just for himself he feels—he feels together with his companions. He takes them into the whole marvelous mosaic he creates. The only criticism I would make is applicable to every great man in football— he does not play for 90 minutes. Giant or not, a man should play for 90 minutes. His actual value? That's incalculable. All I would say is that he is worth the same as Mazzola, who some say is worth 600,000 pounds."

Mario Zagallo, manager of Brazil: "I have no complaints about Best's controversial behavior. If he is handled correctly, it can only do good for the game and its image. He has a Latin temperament. He would easily adapt to our game. In Brazil, tempers fly. Fights and reconciliations are the rule of the day. Best's conflicts with his managers are the fault of the administrators. He has not been allowed to develop fully. I rate him with Moore, Banks, and Pele among the top players in the orld. He is agile, fast, with excellent zigzagging and top-grade footwork. And he has the right temperament."

Ferrucio Valcareggi, manager of he Italian national team: "Without hesitation I place Best in the first five of the world's players. It would not be right to name names but good enough to say these five are the kings of soccer, possibly the greatest the world has ever seen. Best can transform an ordinary match into an epic. The name, the influence he has, are enough. On the other hand, I would not say he is a matchwinner. His colossal technique makes others win the game. That is one of his superb assets. It is difficult to evaluate a man like Best, but I would class him with Angelo Domenghini of Cagliari, and that means he must be worth $800,000.

Billy Bingham, Irish manager of the Greek national team: "Putting prejudice aside, because I used to be his manager, I would say Best is a world player in any position. His biggest enemy is his own temperament. But when he was on the Ireland side with me he was no problem. He gave 100 percent effort. He is a gifted, natural player and this is a tremendous advantage. He has wonderful dribbling control in tight situations near goal. His balance is extraordinary because of his physique. He can shoot equally well with either foot. He is courageous. His passing ability is 90 percent accurate. He can overdo the dribbling—but lately he has improved and is releasing the ball to players who are in better positions. I don't know how much he would be worth now. All I can say is, whatever he gets, then good luck to him!"

It appeared that the day was fast approaching when some sizable offer would be made for George. Besides his purely personal problems, all was not well with the Manchester United team. The team, in large part, retained its glamour image into the '70's with its reputation, and the astonishing luck of Manager Matt Busby's reliance on forward play. In fact, the management and the coaches let things slip badly, long before George departed. Only United's three standout players—Best, Bobby Charlton, and Nobby Stiles— and good fortune obscured the facts that Busby failed to buy new players at the right time and that the youth team failed to produce the caliber of players needed to fill gaps. With Busby as manager and Charlton as captain, United won the European Cup in 1968 in an atmosphere of great emotion. In fact, the United team was weaker but had weaker competition than it had three years earlier when it reached the semifinals, only to lose to Inter-Milan, 3–0. But the 100,000 fans who jammed Wembley in 1968 for the championship game against Benfica didn't give a hoot about that. United's capture of England's first European title, beating the Lisbon team 4–1 in overtime, and the ensuing celebration crowded out any analysis of the victor's underlying problems for a few years.

By 1972, United was in shambles and George was mortified. He recalls "eating my heart out with disillusion at Old Trafford's eventual fall from grace. United should have started to change their side after we'd won the Cup. After that, we started to go downhill slowly. People were getting old and bit by bit things began to turn sour. I could see it coming. I hung on, hoping. Eventually, I had to speak up. Then came the explosion and the rift [over some trades Busby had made]. I suppose I was spoilt at the beginning, but those were some of the unhappiest nights of my life. Each time United got beaten, it was like some national disaster to me. If I'd been a poet I would have felt I had run out of thoughts and words. I got sick of the very game itself. Circumstances defeated me at Manchester United. They were clearing out the old team and they should have let me go as well. But they were frightened of what I might do elsewhere." So he quit.

George did play for other teams during the two seasons after he left United but not on a regular basis. He hooked up with clubs in South Africa and Ireland, then was back to England for a short time playing for Stockport's Fourth Division club. Says George: "The chairman at Stockport was a friend of mine and they were in trouble financially, and he asked me to play to see if I could help out. I did, and in the month I was there, they raised their average gate from around 1,000 to almost 15,000." In retrospect, George calls his early "comeback" efforts jokes played, to make money for myself and to do favors for old friends."

Although he was semi-retired from the game, George kept his run-ins with the law active. In 1974, Marjorie Wallace, Miss World of the previous year, charged George with burglarizing her home, taking a $4,500 fur coat, her passport, and checkbook and had him arrested. Responded George: "That was a false charge. The only thing I ever took from her apartment was what belonged to me —her." The charges were dropped when Wallace failed to show up for the court proceedings.

Early the next year, it appeared that George was ready to start seriously playing soccer again. The New York Cosmos were interested in acquiring him from Manchester United—on the installment plan. The deal was that New York would pay United about $60,000 a month, for George to play from April to August, and would then decide whether to pay another $140,000 to complete the transfer. United Manager Tommy Docherty said: "It is all sunshine to us. We've nothing to lose."

It was all sunshine for Cosmos General Manager Clive Toye, too. After meeting with George in New York, Toye was hopeful: "We told George that by the time he is in his early thirties he would be a multi-millionaire. It will be cash from us and other benefits that come with playing in New York. We want George to play for us and we are prepared to let him combine his two lifestyles—the soccer player and the playboy." Then Toye quipped: "I'll fine him if he is not seen in the nightclubs." Actually, he said it only half-jokingly. What the league needed at the time was a personality, a Joe Namath type who could grab headlines as easily as he made head shots. All seemed well in New York according to George. Said he: "I haven't had any disagreements with them. We are very close. As far as I am concerned there will be no problem. I will be back in two weeks. I am just going over to sort out some things with my business partners."

But there were also other considerations. Later he would explain: "I spent a week in New York discussing terms. I loved the place. But I didn't fancy six months or so living there. It would be too hard. After I turned them down, they got hold of Pele." Not a bad thing to tell the grandkids, if he ever has any.

One day less than a year after he departed New York, George arrived at Los Angeles International Airport. Aztec part-owner Elton John convinced George to come. The date: February 20, 1976. Tinseltown had another glamour boy—Hollywood another star. The flash guns winked, reporters, who had been given sheets of career highlights that listed all the tawdry incidents in George's past, asked their questions. "I'm better than Pele," he jived. "If Pele is worth $4.5 million, I'm worth twice as much with inflation. Yes, most of the things that have been written about me are true, but many of them were blown out of proportion. I'm very happy to get away from the British press and am looking forward to playing football in the United States. I still drink some, but now I'm going to lay off a few days before a game."

A hint of a new George Best? Yes, and there was another; he told the press that he wanted to start training immediately. Within a few weeks Mr. Good Copy himself, the rave of Fleet Street, was as exciting to read about as the local smog conditions.

George later explained his new attitude: "It was important for me to play, and play well, with the Aztecs because I hadn't played hard, competitive soccer for two years. So I went over two months early to train. I had to prove to a lot of people—and most importantly to myself—that I could do it. I knew there were a number of world class players in the NASL, and it would be a tremendous test.

"A few years before, I had felt I could have played in the league and waltzed through, getting by on skills, without being fit. But the league had improved so much. And the standard of play keeps getting higher with people like Pele and all the other European players coming in, inspiring American players to play even better at the same time. The first week or two was full of long runs on the beach. I was so unfit, I would come in a half-mile behind the other lads in a three-mile run. But after five or six weeks, I was as fit as anyone."

The Aztecs and Coach Terry Fisher were impressed. Said Fisher: "Every superstar has a little advantage when it comes to living with rules, but we weren't going to bend them for George. Everybody was going to have the same rules and, as things happened, George never pushed us. He reported to us at 175 pounds and got himself down to 150, which was his playing weight during his prime."

After the season opener, a 2–1 loss to the arch-rival Earthquakes, the team was bused back to its hotel where some local lasses waited to help the Aztecs cope with their defeat. George passed up the chance and talked to reporters: "Ah, it goes by so fast. I could have any one of those women I wanted, but I'm tired of living that way. Don't get me wrong, I still love the young ladies, but now I know what my priorities are. In the two years I was away from the game, I grew up mentally a hell of a lot. All the heavy drinking I did got me in a lot of trouble. I was always staying out all night, sleeping a little during the day, not eating properly, and gambling too much. It was the worst possible way to live. If I was in a bar, I'd have to be the last one out and I'd have to drink more than anybody else. Now I have a new set of values. The only thing that brought me back was my love for the game."

But there was one aspect of it in the NASL that George definitely did not appreciate: the refereeing. Said George: "I can't believe how bad these American referees are. I don't know where they get them. I think they just take the first person who shows up and give him a whistle and cards. It's amazing, they're trying to get the best players here from all over the world and yet they won't get referees. American referees are disgraceful. They don't even know the rules. You're offside when you get the ball, not when it's passed to you. They just disrupt the whole flow of the game. If two men jump for a ball, 99 percent of the time they give a foul against one of them." Or George would add, the refs ignore the most flagrant fouls—shoving, tripping, kicking—committed on him.

"I've been trying to restrain myself," said George, "I've learned to curb my temper off the pitch but sometimes I can't help myself in the heat of a game. Someday I'm just going to blow up and take my best shot at somebody's mouth. I'll get thrown out of the game and probably will be suspended, but if I land my best punch, it'll be worth it. It'll make me feel a lot better."

What made George feel lousy was the Aztecs mediocre play and record. He tried to keep his feelings to himself, but the press, for lack of other compelling stories about George, attempted to flesh out his frustrations. At one point, he simply said, "I'm not a changed person. I want the people to know that I'm here and I don't like to lose, and I'll do everything I can to keep it from happening to our team." Then, after a 2–0 loss in Toronto, a wire service story reported that he was fed up with the team, that he was tired of playing with inferior players and that he probably would leave before the end of the season. George set the record straight in an interview by Fred Robledo of the *Los Angeles Herald-Examiner*. Said George of the story: "It was all a bunch of rubbish. Sure, I was upset with the loss, probably as mad as I've been this year, but I never said I was going to quit. They [reporters] asked me how I felt about the Aztecs and I told them I'd rather not say. That was all there was to the interview. This is the sort of thing that happened with the British press all the time. They would try to read my mind because of something I had said and then went ahead and printed it."

The next splash George made—other than in the Pacific —came when he quit Team America less than a week before the American Bicentennial Cup competition against England, Italy, and Brazil. Though he upset NASL officials, who wanted to show off their best players, including Pele, Bobby Moore, and Rodney Marsh, he had a good reason: "It's because of the way we're playing. After our 6–0 loss to the Cosmos, I decided the Aztecs needed me more than Team America. I've never been on a side that lost 6–0 and that loss hurt me badly. We have two new players arriving from England and I think that it's more important for me to be here and work with them than to play with Team America. They still have many great players and will do quite well without me.

To some that sounded like a lame excuse for wanting time off to enjoy the beach and a little night life. But Fisher attested to George's candor: "George worked harder than ever during that break. People just refuse to believe how determined he was. I knew how much he hated losing and I could see what it was doing to him, but I also knew the rumors about him wanting to leave us were unfounded and that his reason for not playing with Team America was sincere."

George McAlinden, a former United teammate of George's, who shared a three-bedroom beach apartment with him, echoed Fisher: "George has an inner drive that you wouldn't believe. He still thinks he can become as great as he once was and this is his last chance to prove it to himself. He'll let nothing distract him from reaching that goal."

As the season progressed, George became more settled

in his new town, got more accustomed to his new teammates, and regained much of his acceleration. The dazzling
footwork came with more regularity, more authority.
George began performing in a way he was used to, a way
few American observers thought possible.

One play epitomized George's fully flourished talents. In
an important game against Seattle, the Aztecs trailed 3–2
with just three minutes remaining. George took a pass
about 70 yards from the goal and looked up. There was no
route to the goal. Too much opposition. No matter,
George started his game of catch-me-if-you-can. Dribbling
up to one defender, a feint left, a dart right, and George
was past him. A hip fake and a lone fullback warily stands
between ball and goal. With wingers streaking down both
sides, George looks as if he's going to pass off. Instead, he
booms a shot from 23 yards out past the startled goalkeeper. In the tie-breaker, George scored the deciding shot.
George admitted that the tying goal was his finest moment
in American soccer.

After the season (the Aztecs wound up at 12 and 12),
George assessed his comeback: "Now that I know I can
still do it, I know I made the right decision to come to
America. I can't remember any time in my life when I've
been as happy as this summer. Now I'm anxious to return
to England to show those bastards that George Best can
still play football."

George recalled how joining Fulham was decided. "Actually before I went to the States, I spoke with four or five
clubs here at home, sounding out the ground before the
American season ended. A couple of Spanish teams approached me as well as Italian. My personal preference was
for Queen's Park Rangers. I like their style, and I had a
tacit understanding with their chairman that I would welcome Loftus Road if they wanted me. Then suddenly
Fulham sent a couple of emissaries over to Los Angeles for
the Aztecs. The terms they offered were very generous. I
was in a quandary. So I took my problem to a good American friend who knows nothing about football.

"He asked me two simple questions: 'What did QPR do last season?' 'They were runners up in the first division.' 'Where was Fulham?' 'Somewhere in the middle of the second.' 'OK,' came the answer, 'If the Rangers fail to win the title you'll be counted as a failure. On the other hand, if Fulham improves, then you'll have done something.' He, in fact, made up my mind. Now I believe Fulham has the potential to win promotion in a year or two or three. If not, I expect I'll hang myself."

Before George could join Fulham, however, the Football League, described by Joel Powell of the *London Daily Mail* as "an archaic administrative body based in the grimmer North of England," made things difficult for George. Although League officials gave Rodney Marsh and Bobby Moore, who were also returning from America to play with Fulham, little trouble in re-registering, they delayed Best's for weeks. Alan Hardaker, secretary of the League, did not relent until Tommy Trinder, chairman of Fulham and a professional comic, unexpectedly showed up at Hardaker's home and demanded an explanation. Even then, the League put George on probation, giving him permission to play pending a review of his case at the end of the year. George had to prove to League officials that he was "good for the game" and had to show that he "earned" the right to play in England.

It was Hardaker who said, during one of George's difficult periods in late 1972, that he was tired of hearing Best's name. English soccer writer Arthur Hopcraft expressed the sentiments of millions of British soccer fans who had grown disgusted with the League's prissy, headmaster's attitude in dealing with George: "What a deep slough of dismal mean-mindedness is shown by our foremost football official with that wretched comment. Ten thousand Alan Hardakers do not make a minute of football. One hour of Best, at his most glorious, justifies the game and reminds one that it is capable of supreme theatre. If only we have a single George Best, as one remembers him resisting brutal tackles and whipping in a goal with that electric action, we can even carry Alan Hardaker."

The probation arrangement was one last reminder to George that the League did not think kindly of his shuttling back-and-forth across the Atlantic without paying it due deference. More than that, it was a clear sign that League officials would pounce on any indiscretion by George to justify his expulsion. It appeared that he gave them their excuse during Fulham's 4-2 loss to Southampton in October. Disagreeing with a ruling by referee Lester Shapter, George called him a name impugning his manliness and was tossed out of the game. League officials had barely begun to grumble over the incident when Shapter started receiving abusive phone calls and the papers and the public started shouting that George and Fulham were being victimized. Further evidence for the fans came four days later when Bobby Moore was sent off for the first time in sixteen years. Thereupon, public opinion became so strongly in favor of the stars against the bigwigs that the League retreated from George's issue.

Still, the controversy raged. The League, which had accused the Aztecs of "dumping" George on English football for the winter, attacked Fulham for being "arrogant" about the League's desire to know if George would return to Los Angeles. Once more, the fans and the press came to George's defense. Wrote Frank Keating in *The Guardian:* "George Best remains one of the very, very few players with the ability to let sunshine blaze through the dowdy, gray skies of our national game. Indeed, there is cause for the Lancashire pinstripes [League officials] to flop onto their knees and plead with George to stay among us, this Huckleberry who seems to have found his Mississippi down on the lazy, lovely old Thames."

Indeed, all the League had to do was to look at the boost George gave attendance figures in the Second Division. Before they returned, Fulham was averaging 9,437 per game. By the end of the season, it was up to 21,000. On the road too, the crowds came out in huge numbers [by English standards] to see George perform his wizardry. More than 28,000 fans squeezed into Southampton and Sheffield's stadium, while at Swindon, 23,833 turned out to make it the largest gate there in three years. The season's largest crowd to attend a pro match in London, 55,003 at Chelsea, was final proof of George's remarkable drawing power. By the end of the season, this special attraction would pour more than a half million additional pounds in revenue to the Second Division teams.

While the furor over George's return surely helped fill the seats, it was the combination of George and Rodney that was the real hook. Rodney, who had always been just as much a free spirit as George, and twice the comedian on the field, was especially glad to be at Fulham. Said he: "I don't think any other English club and I could have worked out a sensible arrangement. I love to play the game in a way that excites people. That's what we're doing at Fulham and, lo and behold, the rest of the clubs suddenly want some of the same." Of playing with George, Rodney said: "We're important to each other because we need someone else in the team who is on the same wave length, thinking quickly and responding to the unusual. If we're both playing, neither feels lonely when things go wrong. There's nothing George can't do on a soccer field. He's a world class player, a super player. I could have played for other First Division clubs after leaving Manchester United in 1975, but playing with George and Bobby Moore has made the game fun again."

Moore, a former English International captain and 1964 Footballer of the Year, also found that playing with George was exhilarating. Said he: "George has been a pleasure to be associated with. He's one of the most exciting players in the game, and he's proved once again that he can perform his trade at the highest levels. People all over England are anxious to see him playing over here again."

The trio get along so well, in fact, that they often drank, lunched, dined, and partied together. When George was asked whether their fan appeal could be sustained, he kidded, "They'll become genuine Fulham fans when I've scored a few goals." Rodney's response: "That's the trouble with you, George, you take the game too seriously." Even Moore, not the natural charmer that either George or Rodney is, pulled a leg or two. When a housewife approached them in a London pub to ask for their autographs, and said, "It's my son's dream to play alongside you three gentlemen," Moore replied, "I hope he likes plenty of running around."

Their congeniality, however, failed to help much on the playing fields. After a hot start, Fulham faltered and slipped to almost the bottom of the division. Interviewed by a London journalist about the team's plight, George, Rodney, and Bobby drank coffee, tomato juice, and orange squash, respectively, and assessed their team's troubles. "For God's sake," cracked Rod, "don't tell people what we're drinking or it will kill our King's Road image. Let's face it, we had a brilliant start and then I was injured. No, let's be serious. A lot of people thought it was a joke when George and I joined Fulham. Then we put a few good results together and teams started taking us seriously. Some sides thought it was the Cup Final when they met us and players started playing out of their skins." Interjected Bobby: "Rod, there is a bit more to it than that. Let's face it, we have not been playing with the same sort of confidence lately. We are very conscious of being an attacking side. And that often means we are vulnerable to quick breaks. At Forset we held them for 80 minutes and then get stuffed 3–0 in the last 10."

George had his own explanation: "It has been a hard job to put out the same side two weeks running. After a reasonable run we've been hit by injuries and have used four goalkeepers this season. I'm not trying to offer excuses, these are facts."

The three stars were all confident that Fulham would bounce back to avoid relegation to the Third Division (which it did). Said George: "There is a lot at stake for all of us. It is not just a question of fighting our way out of trouble. There is a lot of pride at stake now. But, of course, it has to be a collective effort from all of us. We will fight our way back. A few years ago my attitude might have been a bit different, but I have never played with a better bunch of lads in my life."

George's new maturity showed in a number of ways. One great help was a Miss Angela MacDonald James, a model that George met at a beach party in California celebrating his 30th birthday. They were engaged, split up, and reconciled. . .but even as a rocky relationship, it was a stabilizing influence. Said George: "Let's face it, I'm not the only footballer who enjoys a few drinks and has taken out a few girls. It's up to me what I do. But I have steadied down. I still stare at girls, but Angela gives me hell when she catches me at it. And I must admit I'm pretty possessive about her as well."

Although George had Angela nearby in a fashionable Chelsea flat, he still had a lot of the playboy image. The press gobbled it up and served it a bit, too. George took the gossip in stride: "I don't really think I do anything different than the other guys. But whatever people say criticizing me, it only makes me want to play harder on the field." As in Los Angeles, George was willing to put in the extra time training that his spirited life demanded. "If you're going to play hard off the field, you've got to be prepared to practice hard on the field." When he had a couple of late nights out, he said, "I think I ought to do a little extra work to clean out my system."

A new, mature George Best? For sure. After another smashing season in L.A., he took "the biggest gamble" of his life in Las Vegas—and married Miss James.

RODNEY MARSH

What would Rodney Marsh do if he could not make a living kicking a ball into a goal? "I'd probably be a cat burglar," says the 33-year-old Tampa Bay Rowdy. Would he actually turn to crime in his soccerless life? Oh no, says Rod, "I'd collect cats. I love cats." A small joke, yet vintage Marsh. In what he says and does—especially on a soccerfield, the least one can expect from Rodney is the unexpected. In England, where Marsh grew up as a docker's son in postwar London (he was named after a battleship, the H.M.S. Rodney) and matured, if that's the word, into one of the most dazzling forwards in First Division football, his odd-ball exploits were particularly noticeable. Says Rodney: "Football in England is a gray game, played in a gray country, watched by gray people on gray days."

Rodney just couldn't help but add a big splash of outlandish color. There was the time, for instance, when he picked up the ball in the middle of a match and circled the field with it a couple of times. If you are going to commit a handball infraction, you might as well do something with it. Then there was the road game during which Rodney was getting the treatment from the boo-birds and dropped his pants to show his displeasure with the crowd's behavior. No wonder, then, that the English press dubbed Rodney, "The Clown Prince of Soccer."

And while he has mellowed a bit in the New World—these are, of course, the mellow '70s—Rodney hasn't disappointed his new followers. Here though, where a number of athletes in other sports already had earned the jester's cap, comparisons are more in order. Soccer's Meadowlark Lemon, some sportswriters say. In fact, though, he's more than a globe-trotting jokester. Perhaps he would be best compared to a cross between baseball's Jimmy Pearsall, Mark Fidrych, and Richie Allen—zany, entertaining, and difficult. In his first season with the Rowdies in 1976, Rodney made sure such comparisons would be made; he couldn't let his reputation suffer in America, so he gave one disagreeable referee the same rear view as the crowd in England got. When Boston Minuteman Tom Walsh was assigned to forget the ball during one game and ride Rodney's back instead, pushing him, elbowing him, clinging to Rodney even when the play was in a different part of the field, Rodney stripped off his shirt and strode purposefully to Walsh to hand him the jersey. Walsh refused the offer, and Rodney played the rest of the game with his shirt back on—inside-out. He's even learning the American way of being different. After a game in Fort Lauderdale during the '77 season, Rodney refused to take the team bus back up to Tampa Bay and flew home alone.

Regardless of his iconoclastic personality, Rodney is one of the best in the game. Indeed, he couldn't get away with it if he were a run-of-the-mill player. To put his soccer skills in perspective, one only has to listen to a longtime soccer writer for a London newspaper: "I wouldn't cross the street to see Georgie Best play, but I'd cross an ocean to watch Rodney Marsh."

For sure, Rodney can do things with the ball that just cannot be matched by many other players in the game. If he were to be ranked for flair, he would fall in right behind Pele. If his dribbling skills are surpassed by anyone today, only Best could claim to be his better. As a pure goalscorer, Rodney, when he wants to, can be as unstoppable as Eusebio was in his prime. Although his scoring statistics are not as impressive as some of the game's big guns, it is only one function of another part of sensational game—his passing. Like basketball's Pete Maravich, Rodney is a master of the blind pass, commonly hitting teammates breaking into the open. For the '76 season, Rodney collected 31 points on 11 goals and 9 assists; the following year, he notched 8 goals and 11 assists.

Rodney's value to a team must be measured by more than his scoring figures. In England, where Rodney played pro soccer for fourteen years, he received mixed reviews. After starting with Fulham, he joined Queen's Park Rangers when they played in the Third Division. With Rodney, the team was in the First Division in a matter of two years. Transferred to Manchester City, Rodney was at first a disruptive influence on the cohesive team, and some say he may have cost it an English League title. Yet in the 1975 season, Manchester was captained by Rodney and won the English Cup.

Like so many of the baseball, football, hockey, and basketball stars of North America who have written about their lives for their fans, soccer players in England can count on a wide readership of their autobiographies. In 1976, Rodney came out with his own and the colorful account, *Shooting to the Top,* tells much of the soccer star's early life and personal quirks. Writes Rodney:

"I think it would have been different for me to have become anything but a professional footballer. This is the job for which Destiny ear-marked me the moment I came into the world at Hatfield, in Hertfordshire, as the only son of Bill Marsh . . . He was a docker and a football fanatic . . . He had a lot of skill with the ball, my Dad, and I think if things had gone differently for him early on he could have made the grade as a professional.

"I am sure he saw in me what he would have liked to have been himself. He was determined to give me the opportunity he had missed, and he made sure I had a ball to play with from the moment I could run. Every night we used to go down to the park, sometimes with my uncles, for a kick-about that was always in deadly earnest. My Dad devoted all his time to me and even rain did not stop us: we used to play then in our passage. My Mum knew when to cook our tea.

"An Arsenal home game was a big occasion for us. All the men of the family used to go, about ten in all, and we would walk the three miles to Highbury from our homes in Stoke Newington. I say we walked, but I always made the journey there and back perched high up on the shoulders of my father or one of my uncles. They took it in turn to carry me.

"One of the first matches I went to see was Arsenal against Newcastle, a year or so before Arsenal won the F. A. Cup in 1950. These clubs had great sides then in a great era of football, and the game was a sell-out. Spectators got in over barriers and even a gate was crashed down. It frightened my mother so much that she put her foot down. I was only five years old and first team games, she said, were too much for me. I was only to go to reserve matches.

"There was always television, though, and somebody brought a set into our street. It had a twelve-inch screen with a glass in front that magnified the picture, and people used to come from all over the place to watch a game and our heroes. I don't think anyone forgets the players he worshipped as a kid. I would have loved to have played with them.

"Our house in Stoke Newington wasn't much of a place, but . . . we did have a backyard, and this was another place . . . I used to kick a ball about. I wanted to make the ball do everything, even to speak if possible, and my father showed me a lot of tricks. He could use match-boxes, coins, anything, to flip up and down: all tricks that Ference Puskas, the great Hungarian, impressed everyone when he came to England in 1953. I cannot begin to tell you how much he impressed me. Like my dad, I would practice with anything, oranges, coins, even Bakewell tarts. I would throw a tart up in the air, catch it with a foot and then flick it up again and catch it in my mouth. My concentration was excellent, because I happened to like tarts."

Marsh goes on to describe his first tryout for a team

made up of boys from different schools in his district. "I trotted up to the fellow who was running the trial. 'My name is Marsh,' I said, 'and my teacher told me to play right-half.' 'Where do you want to play?' he asked. 'Inside-left,' I replied. 'Right,' he said, 'full back.' I played for seven minutes!!"

With the district team no longer a possibility, Rodney joined a local boys club, and it was there, he says, "that the foundation of my game was laid. I used to go along almost every night for five-a-side games and, believe me, they were competitive. There were so many squabbles, so much 'needle,' that a player without an edge to his game got nowhere fast."

Rodney's life at that time could not be all football—no schoolboy's life can be—and studies had to play a major part. Says Rodney: "But if football was my big obsession, I did not do badly at school. Some subjects came quite easily, English among them, and I passed my examinations. I could have gone to Hackney Downs Grammar School, but Rugby was their game and the thought of changing my code of football in mid-stream horrified me. So I went instead to Joseph Priestly Technical School and, at age 14, changed to Brooke House Technical College at Hackney.

"Math and subjects like that were a bit of a closed book to me, however, and once during a physics lesson at Brooke House I was caught pencilling in the names of a team for which I was going to play. The master called me out to the front of the class. 'Why do you waste your time with football,' he shouted. 'Football, football, football,' he repeated, waving a blackboard duster in my face. 'You'll never earn your living playing football.' He wrote the same thing on my report. He might have been a good teacher, but he wasn't much of a prophet. I could not get enough football."

Rodney played for three teams—the school's, the district's, and the boys club's—and still managed to find time for his other favorite sports, cricket, table-tennis, and swimming. Looking for young talent, the West Ham team noticed Rodney while he was playing for his district's Under-16 side.

Recalls Rodney: "They invited me to go along for training twice a week, on Tuesday and Friday evenings, under Phil Woosnam and Noel Cantwell. These two players, both big names and both internationals, were first class coaches and they really got through to me. They talked well and with enthusiasm, and they not only knew their subject but they knew how to put it over. I even started playing for West Ham's junior team but this, instead of helping me make progress, led to my break with the club. West Ham received a letter from Sir Stanley Rous, who was then secretary of the Football Association, reminding them that schoolboys were not allowed to play for club teams. That finished me for a short while with West Ham but before I left school they wrote to me asking if I would be resuming training with them on Tuesdays and Fridays.

"This was the moment Fulham came on the scene. They had spotted me playing for Alexander Boys Club and they invited me to play in a trial match. I had a terrible game— I'm the world's worst triallist—yet two days later there was another invitation from them in the post. They wanted me to become an apprentice professional, and for this they were prepared to pay me eight pounds (about $22) a week. It was, as they say, a dream come true.

"West Ham was still interested, but not interested enough to make an offer; and in any case, I knew they had a lot of very talented boys on their ground staff. My dad said Fulham would probably give me better opportunity, and I wanted to go to Fulham because, quite simply, they wanted me."

So they did. At first Rodney would never have guessed that he would grow to love the club, to write that "they were a club in a thousand." Two things about Fulham made it a special team for Rodney: first, "they are a real family club. There is a tremendous feeling of 'togetherness' (among the players). Secondly, "I was always aware of the tremendous spirit in the dressing room. It was sort of a natural conspiracy by the players against the knocks of fate. They were serious about their football, but they could laugh at themselves as easily as they could laugh at trouble, and when people enjoy life the impossible does not seem so difficult."

It was this great affection for the team that enabled Rodney to fondly recall his difficult start with Fulham. "My first day at Fulham, as a 16-year-old back in 1961 was far from ordinary. I was 20 minutes late in reporting and less than an hour later I was involved in a fight—no punches pulled—with one of the other ground staff boys. I travelled from Stoke Newington to Fulham by tube and the first person I met was Jack Gordon who was in charge of the ground staff. 'Welcome,' he said 'You'll be sweeping the stands.' I don't really know what I expected, but it was certainly not that. There were about eight boys and each was given a specific job. The lucky one went to the dressing room while others went on to the terraces, the track or the stands. I climbed up into the main stand where another lad was already at work. 'You're late,' were his first words. 'You sweep over there, and don't forget, you've got some to catch up on me.'

"Somehow, he got right under my skin and the next moment we were lying about each other in a way that suggested only one of us would come out of it alive. It was a fight with a bit of real hate in it that even saw us, locked together, rolling down the steps of the stand. Some of the other boys fortunately saw what was happening and ran over to break it up. It was a fine start to my career as a professional footballer!"

As much as Rodney is known for his antics on the field, he has plenty of off-the-field quirks, too. Says he: "I am glad that no psychologists have been around in recent seasons to watch me getting ready to leave home for a match, because they would probably have certified me on the spot. What other action could they have taken on seeing me stuff a tiny, toy rabbit into one pocket, putting sunglasses into another, even though it might have been raining outside, making sure I had a little gold charm in yet another pocket and a medallion round my neck and then picking up a large koala bear, another toy, before leaving? Yet the explanation is quite simple, or at least I think it is. I am superstitious, you see, though I must also add that I do not believe in the power of superstition to make me play better. I am sure it has never brought me good luck, but I feel that if I don't carry my bits and pieces then I may have bad luck. I refuse to take a chance."

In any event, Rodney does not believe that in the matter of superstitions, at least, he is any different from other athletes. Says Rodney: "Football is riddled with superstition, more so probably than any other sport, and there are few players who haven't got a little trinket in their pocket or some special routine to follow just before a match. They may not talk about it, but, believe me, it is important to them." Some of these superstitions are very simple, like putting on the left boot first, or sitting in a particular corner of the changing room or running out in a certain position when the team takes field."

One English player's superstition took, says Rodney, a less obvious form. "Jimmy Langley always refused to touch the ball in the changing room before a match. He would be wild if he did, and Alan Mullery used to play on this in their Fulham days. Alan is a great niggler, and he would get hold of a ball and start kicking or throwing it at Jim. Jim used to leap all over the place, trying to avoid it." Rodney's interests outside of soccer include art and reading. "I am not an expert, not by a long chalk," he says, "but I have had many hours of pleasure just looking at paintings, reproductions in books as well as originals. I particularly admire the French impressionists, Renoir, Cezanne and so on, but my taste is very catholic and if a painting appeals to me it doesn't matter whose signature is on the bottom."

While Rodney's reading horizons have no doubt expanded, he has written about one of his most pleasurable experiences: "For a long time, I had a love affair with just one book. This was Pear's Cyclopedia, that wonderful collection of facts and figures. I used to spend most of my travelling time reading it, taking in all sorts of curious statistics that used to come in handy when we had quizzes —another handy, less individual, way of passing time on long journeys. I even wrote up to Pear's once complaining about what I thought was a contradiction in a note about Apollo, the Greek god. I got an indignant reply explaining that it was my understanding of the note, not the note itself, that was wrong!"

While Rodney had been the Manchester City captain, that, too, was wrong for him, and he was not happy to be on the transfer list when Tampa Bay General Manager Beau Rogers began pursuing him. Says Rodney: "At Manchester City in '75, I spent four or five months not playing. I'd had a tremendous bust-up with management and I was having trouble with my personal life as well. I had a nervous breakdown and had to go to the hospital for three weeks. It all started over an argument over tactics; it was very stupid." Perhaps fortunate, too. Early in 1976, Rogers' wooing finally resulted in Rodney choosing to leave England. "I made this decision on the spur of the moment," he said. "I was becoming a little bit sick of inactivity." A $300,000 contract for the Rowdies' six-month season helped to make the move a bit more attractive.

Hoping to leave his reputation as a loon behind him, Rodney still knew that he was expected to do more than just play top rate soccer. Said G. M. Rogers: "One of the reasons we wanted him is because he's a showman. We're in the entertainment business, and he's got a certain flair. He combines that flair with tremendous skill. And if he wants to turn it on, he could be the Pied Piper of American soccer."

At first, Rodney's flamboyance was held in check. At his first meeting with the American press, he was asked what the Rowdies would have to do to build their team around him. "That's not right," responded Rod. "It's me who has to fit in with the team." Later he would add, "I like being not recognized over here. I like to be alone. But to be a good professional footballer it shouldn't matter. He should do as well in front of 2 people as 100,000. He should take pride in his performance and I've got that. It will take a while for people to know who Rodney Marsh is, but I don't mind. In America, you're still selling the game, much less the players."

For the Rowdies Coach Eddie Firmani, who has since moved to the Cosmos, Rodney would sell himself with his play. "There's no question about it," said the coach, "he's one of the most skillful players in the world. They've tried to stereotype him over in England into the typical English player. In America, Rodney Marsh will be allowed to be himself. You see him at practice, and he does lag about a bit, but suddenly he's down the field with the ball. You don't build a team around him, but at the same time you cannot tie his hands behind his back, and Rodney's an artist at what he does."

Blending into the Rowdies without losing his crowd-pleasing panache proved a difficult task for Rod, but he managed to pull it off without too much trouble for himself. He adapted to the Florida suncoast easily enough, zipping around the area in his Jaguar and showing up regularly at Boneshaker's, the team's after-game watering hole. His family—wife Jeanne, daughter Joanna, son Jonathan —joined him and Rodney could show the "real me." For Rodney, that means, "I go home to the family, have an occasional beer and watch a lot of TV. My life is very slow, and I like it that way. I'm a very peaceful and placid person. It takes a lot to get me upset. I like to lounge around in denims and just relax." What particularly pleased him about America, besides the "pop-pop-fizz-fizz-oh-what-a relief-it-is" commercial, was its contrast to staid England. "What's the use of coming thousands of miles and have nothing different. I might as well have stayed home."

Returning to England after the '76 Rowdies closed with a disappointing semifinal playoff defeat, 2–0 to Toronto,

Rodney, in fact, almost did stay home. During the off-season, Rodney was sold back to the English League's second division Fulham club with the proviso that he be available on loan for three seasons. Firmani was not informed of the deal and, in any event, had enough of trying to work the Marsh style into the Rowdies' approach. When Rodney joined the team in '76, Firmani noted that, "If you try to knock his flair out of him and tell him to do certain things that a player like him shouldn't be doing, then there could be a certain bit of animosity between coach and player." Firmani, as it turned out, had no personal enmity for Rodney but just figured that the team would do well enough without the clown prince. Firmani felt strongly about it and threatened to quit if Rodney was brought back—and so, one winter day in London, Rodney was apprised of the turn in his American career by a blaring headline: "Marsh Sacked By Tampa."

Within two weeks, however, the Rowdies reversed their decision. Rogers pointed out to Firmani some contractual obligations involving Rodney and asked if Firmani would have him back if Rodney would promise to follow orders. After a long distance phone conversation between the coach and the player, Firmani reconsidered. Said Rodney: "I read that headline and was shocked. I thought I had played well in my last two games last year and had left on a high note. Then came the turnaround. I don't know why Eddie changed his mind, but I am glad he did, all right. I am ready to play as he wants."

What Firmani wanted was simply more play and less entertaining. Rodney honestly appraised the request. "I'll be the first to admit I got mixed up last year between entertaining and working. That was my doing. Eddie wants me to work first and entertain second. I'll do that. I'm not paid for entertaining if we are losing. This year the job is to win."

The '77 season for Rodney thus started on the right foot. No longer would he have the added pressure of the captaincy to deal with—he had resigned from the post early in

'76. No longer would the high salary he was drawing be a spark of a players' move to get a bonus pay system. No longer would the feisty Stewart Scullion be there to trade angry words—he had been traded in the off-season. No longer would Rodney in his forward position be able to dally, as was his wont occasionally—he would pull back to midfield at times to get more involved in the play.

A "New Rodney Marsh," Bay Area papers said, but '77 would hold its own problems for Rodney. His marriage broke up, his children were on the other side of the big pond. Said Rodney: "You can get over a woman— but you can't get over losing your own flesh and blood. You get a lump in your throat talking to your kids on the phone, across the Atlantic, knowing you're not going to see them for a long time."

Rodney also had to deal with his growing reputation in America. While trying to play the role of team man, his eccentric individuality could not be suppressed. Some suggested that he was simply nuts. Rodney's response: "They said the same thing about Beethoven, Tschaikovsky and Van Gogh. The dividing line between genius and insanity is a very fine line. Unfortunately, I'm on the other side of it."

Gordon Hill, the renowned former English referee and the Rowdies director of community development, defended Rodney: "As a schoolmaster in England, I always tried to come to grips with this problem of the exceptional child, whether it be in academics or athletics. The problem is that the world aspires to mediocrity. To be seen as different from that makes you an oddball. This produces one of two reactions—one retort is to conform and become mediocre as well. The other is to exaggerate that uniqueness, to go out on a limb." Retorts Rodney: "That's me. My anti-establishmentism, anti-authoritarianism was a conscious thing. I've always been against conformity for conformity's sake. I'm unpredictable. I'm totally consistent in my inconsistency. Everything I do is there for everybody to see. And it isn't only soccer, it's my life. My life is an open book. If I make a mistake, I may go out and get drunk, but I don't hide in my room drinking. I don't go around in alleys with women on the road. In my case, you can make up your own mind. You either love me or hate me."

More important to Rodney than the public's acceptance of him was the need to build better relations with his teammates. Rodney explained that his career has been "very turbulent because of my inability to accept second best. I've been very intolerant of managers, coaches and players. But in the last two years, I've grown to become more tolerant. I'm more mature. In the past, playing with inferior players infuriated me. I would get angered by other's mistakes. That's probably why I've been unpopular. I didn't have the ability to adapt myself to their limitations."

That is what he wants his teammates to do for him. Near the close of last season, Marsh reflected on the matter: "I'm still not accepted totally by all the other players. What more can I do? I'm not a very good worker up front. I'm more of a drifter. But I would be nice if players accept my limitations. I accept theirs. I accept that Farrukj Quraishi can't cross the ball with his left foot. I accept that Lenny Glover will never score another goal for the rest of his life. Why can't they accept my limitations?"

Harsh, perhaps, and a touch melodramatic, but who said Rodney Marsh was anything else. At 33, he's not about to change appreciably, though he may ripen a bit. Looking ahead, Rodney likes to think that an offer to coach in America will come his way. If so, he knows how he would handle a player in his own mold—"let him do what he does best, let him totally on his own." Among other professional ambitions, Rodney would like to manage a winning U. S. World Cup team. A pipe dream maybe, but Rodney Marsh has been known to surprise soccer fans with remarkable regularity. At this point in his career, the only real surprise would be if he faded into obscurity—or, of course, if he became a cat burglar.

JIM McALISTER

At Portland's Civic Stadium, there were about 10 minutes left in the NASL championship game. A few minutes earlier, Georgio Chinaglia had scored on the Seattle Sounders to put the New York Cosmos ahead for good, 2–1. The Sounders began peppering New York with shots —all near-misses or saved by goalkeeper Shep Messing. At the other end of the field, the action was slow. For Sounder left back Jim McAlister, it was time to make his move. The 20-year-old defender sidled up to Pele and popped his question. He simply wanted to know whether after the game he could have Pele's jersey. He got his wish. Said Jim: "It was a very emotional thing for me, it being his last league game ever. It was a true honor."

So too was the Rookie of the Year award that NASL players voted Jim. Though only 5 ft. 8 in. tall and 140 lbs., Jim played his left back position with the aplomb of a seasoned vet. As proof of the fact that he wasn't given the award just because he was the best *American* rookie, he also was selected as an honorable mention on the league's All-Star team. Clearly, he is one of the NASL's outstanding defensemen. Said his coach, Jim Gabriel: "Jimmy's as good as anyone there is, and if he went anywhere in the world he'd be given a chance to play."

Jim got his first opportunity to play as a seven-year-old in West Seattle, not very far from the Sounders' Kingdome. It was his father who got him started in the game on a regular basis. Said Jim: "My dad was the athletic director at our school, and they had a soccer team of mostly 11- and 12-year-olds. They didn't have enough players, so they put me out there. I was only in the second grade, but I played anyway. In my neighborhood, soccer was all there was. We all played. There always were pickup games at Hiawatha Park. We had a team called the Hammers and one year we went 33-0 with a couple of ties. Soccer was my game."

Still, Jim played baseball and kicked field goals in high school. Not that he had given up on soccer, but rather, he was already involved on a higher level. At 13 he had signed with a local senior league team, eventually playing for the Olympia Vikings, a club sponsored by the famous Northwest brewery. It was there that he switched from playing center forward and midfield to the back line.

Jim's sterling play for the Vikings was spotted by Sounders' scout Jimmy Johnston, who soon was on the phone to the youngster. "I remember Jimmy asked me my height and weight when he called. I said, 'No, don't ask me that.'" Fortunately, Johnston was savvy enough about soccer to know that size doesn't mean that much, that Jim's skills would more than make up for his lack of bulk.

Jim picked up those skills simply by playing a lot. He learned quickly that to become good no easy short-cuts could be taken. "Soccer is a sport you must work hard at," he says. "There are so many facets of the game. The main thing when you're young is to learn how to control the ball with your feet, thighs, and chest. It's all a matter of practice. You try to never get discouraged; it's like anything else you want to learn well. And if you do want to get good at it, there are going to be times when you get pissed off at yourself and feel like quitting. But you have to work hard every day and put your mind and heart into it and say to yourself, 'I want to get good at it.' "

While Jim learned the basics by playing, he also picked up a lot about the game by watching the pros play. He and friends journeyed to Vancouver to catch closed circuit TV games from England. When the occasional soccer tour came through Seattle, Jim was there, too. One of his favorite players was Clyde Best, now with Portland, who visited Seattle with his West Ham team. Even now, he has special players he likes to watch. Best is still one. Others are George Best, Franz Beckenbauer, and teammate Mike England.

During the 1976 season Jim was used on the Sounders' reserve squad and played a total of 96 minutes. The next year would be different. "I knew I would make the traveling squad," said Jim, "but that wasn't enough. I wanted to play." He did, starting 21 games, missing two because of a concussion he suffered in a home game against the Cosmos and another couple because of the some lineup experiments that Gabriel made. As the season progressed, Gabriel was forced to make one more shift that would set Jim in his left back position. With Sounder veterans England and Paul Gillete and English star Mel Machin entrenched in the defensive alignment, Gabriel moved team captain Adrian Webster up to midfield.

The chance to play in his most natural position helped Jim hone his skills. His coach and teammates were impressed. Said Gabriel: "He had a super season for us. Even though some experienced players weren't performing at their best, Jimmy never stopped hustling. He has it all. He is great in the air and can jump higher than anyone else on the club, in spite of his height. He is going to be a tremendous fullback." His line mates could not agree more. Said Machin: "Jimmy learns so quickly that it won't be long before there aren't any fundamentals left to show him. At times, he's been absolutely brilliant." Added English: "Jimmy listens. He wants to learn. You tell him something once and you don't have to tell him again. It's a simple game and Jimmy does the simple things right. First, he's learned the basics and applies them. He doesn't try to impress by getting too clever. Second, he compensates for a lack of physical size and strength with skill and intelligence — the trademarks of a class defender." Those who play with and against Jim, moreover, point out that he has a certain talent that few young players have: the ability to "read" the game. By this they mean that he can sense the flow of the game, where his teammates and opponents are and where they are heading, as well as the probable movement of the ball. For a defender, this aptitude is essential for both containing opposing attackers and, once in possession of the ball, for finding the best route by which to clear it. No doubt, it was Jim's early exposure to the game and his constant practice that gave him this sixth sense.

There is one particular aspect of the game, however, that Jim believes he has yet to master. Says he: "My weakness is in attacking. I like to attack but at times don't feel comfortable doing it. Experience is the key: when to do certain things and when not to. I haven't attacked enough. There is more interchanging in soccer today. You have to be able to play every position well."

In the off-season, Jim conducted numerous clinics in the Seattle area's schools and became a regular on the banquet circuit. He continued to live at home with his mother—Jim's dad died in 1974—and managed not to let his newly found fame upset things with his steady girl friend.

Among Jim's ambitions now is to be able to settle accounts with the Cosmos. After the championship game defeat, he sat in the subdued dressing room, tears streaming down his face, and said, "There's no doubt we're the better *team*. We attacked the whole game, but it just wasn't meant to be, today." Some months later the loss still haunted him. "I'm looking forward to seeing the Cosmos again," he said. "This time the score will be different." That remains to be seen, but one thing is almost certain: some day, somewhere, some kid will ask for Jim McAlister's jersey.

STEWART SCULLION

Although he stands only 5 feet, 7 inches tall and weighs just 155 pounds, Portland Timber forward Stewart Scullion is as tough as they come. One reason is that he almost always had to be. From his early childhood until he was 14, Stewart lived in an orphanage in Bathgate, Scotland, and spent much of his time watching out for his younger sister Jeanette and brother John. About the only advantage in the situation was that Stewart had plenty of time to begin developing his soccer skills. "There were a lot of playing fields at the orphanage," he says. "That's really all we had to do. We played every day, sometimes until nine or ten o'clock at night."

When the three Scullion kids were adopted by a woman in London, Stewart continued his playing in the city schools. At age 16, he quit his education and took up a profession. It was not as an apprentice on one of the professional soccer clubs which searched for young prospects. Instead, he worked in the accounting office of British Airways, keeping up his soccer with the company team and a local amateur squad. Recalls Stewart: "Playing professionally hadn't occurred to me. I had had a funny life. I never won any honrs. I just played the game and enjoyed it."

Two years later, in 1964 when Stewart was 18, he thought otherwise and signed a pro contract with Charlton. "I felt that if I'm good at something, I might as well try to make a living at it." One of the club's players was Eddie Firmani, who, years later, as coach of the Tampa Bay Rowdies, would offer Scullion his first NASL contract. Their early crossed paths was purely coincidental to that. Says Stewart: "I never really got to know Eddie. He was a senior pro, and I was only a kid, a groundstaff boy. People always ask me if that's why Eddie brought me to Tampa. It really didn't have anything to do with that because I never knew him."

Within a year, Stewart was traded to Watford in the Third Division, was immediately put into the first team and held the spot for nearly seven years. The Watford manager then was Ken Furphy, who also would do a stint as a coach in the NASL for the New York Cosmos. Says Stewart, "I think he saw me play well once against the Watford reserves, and they were looking for a winger at the time. I play up front more now, but at that time I used to stay wide. I created more goals than I scored."

In Stewart's first two years at Watford, the club barely missed promotion to the Second Division. The second season, Watford finished just out of the money when only the two top teams were promoted. The next year, it won the Third Division championship and made it to the semifinal of the Football Association Cup, the first time a Third Division team had ever gotten that far in F. A. Cup competition.

The next year in the Second Division was a particularly hard one for Stewart and the Watford side. "We struggled," Stewart remembers, "and I felt it was the toughest league I ever played in. Everyone is just one division from the top, so they try all the harder for promotion."

Stewart joined the First Division in 1971 when he was bought by Sheffield United for 30,000 pounds, or roughly $60,000 at the time. In preseason training, Stewart made the first team and stayed on it for the entire year. In the very first match of the following year, however, calamity struck. Stewart collided with Welsh centerhalf Johnny Roberts, and by the time the dust settled, he had a broken leg, a torn cartilage in one of his knees, and a fractured wrist. The mishap forced Stewart out of the lineup for most of the season. "It was just one of those things," says Stewart. "I did play the last ten games, but I wasn't fit."

The next year, 1973, Stewart was still having trouble with one of his injuries. "My knee kept swelling up. I played up to Christmas, but I was in a rut and not playing well." Sheffield United's management must have noticed that too, for it dealt Stewart back to his first club, Watford —not exactly a step ahead in the young scorer's career.

During the 1974 season, Stewart first learned of the possibility of continuing his playing in America. Recalls Stewart: "A friend told me Eddie Firmani was looking for players to come to America, and I asked him to put a word in for me. The next week Eddie gave me a call. [Sheffield United's manager] Mike King was great; he let me sign a contract with Tampa."

At last free from the aftereffect of his injury, Stewart came to the United States in the spring of '75. With him were his wife Rita, and sons, Darren and Russell. Playing the Cosmos in his NASL debut, Stewart scored the only goal in Tampa Bay's 1–0 victory. The rest of the season progressed just about as well for Stewart and the Rowdies. The team took their conference and won the NASL championship by defeating the Timbers, 2–0.

Stewart scored ten goals during the '75 campaign and picked up eleven in the next year, as the Rowdies once more won the Eastern Division title. In both years, Stewart was named to the NASL all-star second team. Perhaps Stewart's greatest value to the team was his passing ability. The Rowdies' top scorer Derek Smethurst got many of his goals off feeds from Stewart.

It shocked the league, then, when the Rowdies sold Stewart to the Timbers before the start of the '77 season. One reason given at the time was that Rodney Marsh, the Rowdies' temperamental, zany star, and Stewart did not get on all that famously on the field. In any event, Stewart was not much surprised. Said he: "I had a feeling they

[Portland]would try to buy a new team since they didn't win it in '76. It was just a case of not being wanted in one place and being wanted somewhere else. Of the negotiations with the Timbers, Stewart says, "It was first class all the way. It was all done verbally in a short time."

Early in the '77 season, Stewart had high hopes for the team. Said he: "If we keep everybody fit and get to the playoffs, it will take a good club to beat us. Considering the points we've gotten in spite of all our injuries, I've got no grumbles. The big thing is we're a team. When we win, it's 16 players winning, not just those on the pitch. Coach Brian Tiler treats people equally. He has the same respect for those on the bench as he does for those playing."

Unfortunately for Portland, the injuries (including a couple to Stewart) hurt the team gravely, and it wound up in the Western Division cellar. Still, Scully, as Stewart is called by his teammates, came on in the second half of the season to score nine of his eleven goals. With three assists, he wound up with twenty-five points.

After the playoffs concluded, Stewart joined the New York Cosmos on a two-month tour of South America, Asia, and Europe to mark Pele's retirement from the game. Eddie Firmani, who had left the Rowdies to lead the Cosmos to the league championship, by then knew Stewart quite well from Tampa Bay, so it was no coincidence that they would team up again. Firmani was well aware of how tough a player Stewart was and how valuable he'd be on the grueling tour.

Indeed, around the league, Stewart is considered one of the fiestiest and most determined players in the game. He believes his grit may well come from his early years in Scotland. Says Stewart: "In those days I never had nothin'. I never knew what pocket money was. I learned you have to work for what you get. So I work hard to give my wife and boys a good living. It won't change because I still have those scars from the orphanage. If I had to dig the roads for a living, I'd do it—just to make sure my boys have it better than I did."

GORDON BANKS

"I just couldn't believe it. It was the greatest save that I have ever seen, by the greatest goalkeeper I have ever faced. I will never know how he managed it. To me it was not possible." Pele's remembrance of Gordon Banks' spectacular stop in England's 1970 World Cup match against Brazil in Mexico is shared by millions of soccer fans around the world. Television stations in 26 countries were bombarded with requests for replays of the astounding play. Indeed, of reports kept, that one moment of sporting action was probably seen by more people more times than any other single athletic feat in history.

For sure, soccer nuts of the global village will always recall that July 7 with special reverence. It was a 100-degree day in Guadalajara when the blessed deflection was made before 75,000 fans in Jalisco Stadium. The matchup of England and West Germany had, in itself, ignited great interest among the sport's followers. For starters, there was Pele, the greatest forward of all-time going up against England's Bobby Moore, then considered the best defender around, bar none. Then there were a sharp contrasts in the teams' styles and attitudes: the reticent, unsmiling, defensive English against the ebullient, daring Brazilians.

Eleven minutes into the game, which until that point had

been largely in England's control, Carlos Alberto (now a New York Cosmo) gave the ball along the right side to Jairzinhoh, and the winger sped past his defender towards the goal line. From there, he centered the ball past the near post of the goal where Banks was correctly positioned. The pass, like a perfectly aimed chip shot, was coming down near the far post about seven or so yards out. Moving like only he seems to do, Pele rose in one of his great stretching leaps, arched his back and neck to get behind and above the ball and connected with a typically smashing header. Banks, it appeared to all, was hopelessly stranded. Pele's header, fast and aimed perfectly toward the far post looked like a sure thing. As one English defender was to say later, Pele was shouting "goal" almost as soon as the ball flew off his head. The crowd, too, rose to its feet, as if following Pele's lead and began cheering the goal.

Then Banks worked his magic. With a burst of speed that left everyone who saw it in absolute awe, the goal-keeper hurtled himself across the goalmouth. The dive was so fast that is seemed to negate the basic laws of physics and gravity. More than that, Banks managed, while in the air, to twist his body and fling out his right hand just as Pele's shot was bouncing hard off the turf just two or three feet from the goal line. With the top of his hand, Banks deflected the ball up and over the crossbar and hit the ground with a dusty thump.

Banks' move instantly throttled the crowd into silence. Pele stopped dead in his tracks, shook his head in disbelief and stared at Banks as the goalkeeper sat, at first solemn, and then laughing on the ground. Then Pele in an un-mistakable salute to Banks, shot his right arm into the air.

How did Banks do it? The speed of the save was such that Banks himself, afterward, was not sure where exactly he had hit the ball; at first, he said he caught it at shoulder height, then changed his story to say that he tipped it at thigh height. In fact, he reached it just as it was coming off the turf—no more than a foot or two above the ground. Later, Banks would attempt to explain what was, no doubt, his totally instinctive maneuver. Said he: "All I could do was guess how hard it would bounce and what speed it was likely to come off the pitch. I knew I couldn't reach it, but I thought I might be able to touch it with one hand."

For Banks, full realization of the impact, of the save, on his life only began to sink in after the English returned home. The trip back to London was not a happy one for the team nor, particularly, for the goalkeeper. After losing to Brazil 1–0 in the game that Banks made his great save, England qualified for the quarter final round by ousting Czechoslovakia. The night before the game with West Germany, Banks came down with severe stomach pains and dizzy spells after having a bottle of beer and could not recover sufficiently to play—so he had to watch while his mates built a two-goal lead five minutes into the second half only to have it tied by a goal in the closing minutes by Uwe Seeler. In overtime, German's scoring ace Gerd Muller put in the game winner. After the loss, Banks, always tough on himself, berated himself for not trying to play regardless of his illness. What made the loss especially trying for Banks was that his last-minute replacement, Peter Bonetti, was blamed for two of the three German goals.

Banks' self-reproach soon passed after he saw the welcome that he received upon returning. Crowds mobbed him at the airport, his fan mail tripled, and the management of Banks' Stock City team had to make a public appeal to stem the flood of requests for personal appearances by Banks throughout the country. The incredible save was the talk of the nation for months. Banks, already a sports celebrity and long considered one of the game's greatest goalies in history, became the personification of England's unique spirit when faced with defeat.

For those who knew Banks well, it came as little surprise that his newly enhanced fame failed to change the man very much. He remained the totally dedicated footballer, somewhat shy and always ready, it seemed, to break into the broad, toothy grin that helped to nickname him Fernandel,

after the French film comic. Still, the save became the key-
stone of the Banks legend in much the same way Willie
Mays' over-the-head catch of Vic Wirtz's long drive in the
1954 World Series epitomized the Say Hey Kid's career.
Says Banks: "What that save did was give me a label. People think of me as the man who made the save on the great
effort by Pele. It is a wonderful feeling to be recognized for
something like that. People who have seen hundreds of
games and love soccer seem to remember that save above
all else. For me to have been involved, and for it to have
been against the greatest player I've ever seen is very special. When I see it even now, I get a thrill; it gets better and
better." Nonetheless, the play did create one minor problem for Banks. He says: "The only thing I resent about
people continually bringing up that save is that I've made
many others I consider its equal."

If the miracle save represented the pinnacle of Banks'
playing career, the deepest valley for him came not on a
playing field but on a narrow road near his home in Staf-
fordshire, England. One wet Sunday afternoon in October
1973, Banks was driving home when his attempt to pass on
the country lane ended in a head-on collision with a van.
Shards of glass from the windshield embedded in his face
and right eye. Rescuers found him wandering around the
wreck of his car holding one hand to his battered eye. The
doctors used 108 stitches to mend Banks' face, but there
was nothing medically possible to be done to save the eye.
In the prime of his career—one that had seen him represent
England 73 times in international matches; that had seen
him yield only three goals in six games as England swept to
the World Cup at Wembley in 1966; that had produced
that greatest save ever—Banks' future in the game was
most seriously imperiled.

In the hospital for two months, Banks was inundated
with the attention that a national hero deserves, although
some of it was less than fully appreciated by him. Recalls
Banks: "I had literally thousands and thousands of cards
and gifts. Radios. Chocolates. Bottles of whiskey. Friends

smuggled in beer. We had a rather complete bar. Reporters were trying to beat each other to the story coming from my own mouth. I didn't want to talk to anyone. One reporter tried to bribe a guard to get to see me and two others were caught climbing over the wall near my room. The funniest incident occurred when I was having a TV set delivered to my room. I was there just under a week and had no visitors at that point. One fellow came in wearing white overalls and asked me where I'd like the TV. As I was telling him, two others came in with the set and asked where to put it. When they left, the first chap said, 'I'm from the *Daily Express.*' I got him thrown out. I didn't want to talk about it at that point.''

Nor did Banks really want to consider how the injury would affect his career as goalkeeper. Obviously, good eyes are essential for athletes, but for goalkeepers, they are as important as sound legs are for forwards. Of course, Banks was used to playing in less than top condition. As the number one goalie in Europe for years, he had taken a lot of punishment from forwards who believed that fouling was probably the best way of handling him. Banks' hands, in particular, received constant beating. Gnarled and bent out of shape, though surprisingly soft and small for a goal-keeper, Banks' hands have suffered from broken bones and dislocations on almost a regular basis. Three of his fingers are permanently deformed and, somehow or other, he lost the knuckle on the small finger of his left hand. Banks, in typical matter-of-fact attitude to the harsh physical re-alities of soccer, says, "You play with so many injuries which never get a proper chance to heal."

As with his other injuries, Banks never complained pub-licly about his lost right eye, but after three months of con-valescence, promises of comeback dates, and some early attempts to play, he finally accepted the fact that he was finished with world-class football. He had told himself that he could follow the ball while watching games on TV, but out on the field he found that his vision was blurred, and his distance perception was distorted. An announcement—unemotional and to the point—was made that Banks would retire as an active player. At home, however, he wept.

Banks stayed on with the Stokes team, then a leading First Division team, and devoted himself to coaching. He was also made comanager of England's Under-23 team, but it was evident to all that he sorely missed the day-to-day involvement that he had with the game as a player. He played in pick-up games, charity matches, and almost any contest that would have him. The "friendly matches" told Banks what he wanted to know: he was able to play again.

The adjustment was difficult. Said Banks: "At first I'd be pouring tea and missing the cup entirely. The specialist said the other eye would take over eventually. But when I tried to play again, I had trouble with distance, with finding the ball. It would be on top of me before I realized. I didn't give myself long enough to practice before making the decision." The decision to retire.

As Banks regained confidence in his game, he learned that his longtime friend Ron Newman was looking for a new goalkeeper for the Ft. Lauderdale Strikers, the offspring of the Miami Toros. Newman approached Banks about assuming a position of player–coach, and the idea made loads of sense to Banks. Forging a comeback at age 37 is no easy task for any athlete, and when the player was once considered the top at his position and had a serious physical problem to contend with, attempting the return away from the scrutiny of his closest followers seemed a logical way of doing it.

When Banks arrived at Florida, one club official remarked that he didn't think the new goalkeeper would be "much of a factor on the field." The restrained expectations were exactly what Banks wanted. Said he: "I didn't think I could live up to the standards I had set back home. If I can't live up to it here, people won't be saying, 'I remember him when.' I just felt that playing in itself is what

I wanted to do. It was something that was missing in my life. I felt my career had been cut short, and I wanted to see if I could relive it a bit."

While Banks was ready to give everything he had within himself to making the comeback a success, he had to be honest about the limitations that his halved vision created. He said, "Obviously, a dimension has gone. I can put my hand up on one side and I can't see it. And in certain situations when I have to concentrate on a player with the ball quite close to the goal, I can't see other fellows who are running up into potential striking positions. So I have to read the game better than I did. I have to allow for a quick look around and judge whether or not I can cover if the man with the ball releases it to another forward. I've always explained the situation to whomever I've played with, so that they'll come in and help me out in a way that they might not with another goalie. They realize I can compensate with the experience I have in other ways."

One of the reasons that Banks also chose to make his comeback in the NASL rather than in England's First Division was that the league would not insure a goalie with one eye. League officials said the risks of injury were too high in such a case. Banks, himself, knew full well that he might be endangering the healthy parts of his body. Said he: "I take that chance every time I play. I know that I cannot see someone coming in from my blind side if I'm charging a man with the ball. But my defenders know in what situations it might occur."

Judging by Banks' first season in the NASL, he got along just fine in the goal and with his defensive teammates. Of his first games for the Strikers, Banks said he was "very nervous. I think I was as nervous as I was before my first game in the First Division when I was 20." But Banks nevertheless was happy not to have to restart his pro career in the role of supercelebrity. Banks said: "It takes a lot of weight off your shoulders. I won't miss the finger-pointing kind of thing. I wasn't the kind of person who liked that, anyway."

What Banks did, and always will, like is winning. At Ft. Lauderdale the pressure that would have accompanied a comeback in England may not have been present, but the old professional drive to win was as strong as ever. Banks' vision may have been limited, but his ability to read the flow of play in front of him, his leadership of the defense, and his instinctual ability to position himself correctly were all as strong as ever. In the first nine games of the season, he allowed only twelve goals and only for half of those could he be held primarily responsible. By the time the season was two-thirds over, it was clear that the Strikers' 10–6 record was, in great measure, due to the tough team defense led by Banks. The official who doubted that Banks could make much of a contribution to the team was not signing another team: "He's kept us in a lot of games this season."

Strikers' Coach Ron Newman, who never had doubted what Banks could do, was more open about the goalkeeper's worth to the team. Said Newman: "Some of the saves he's made couldn't have been done better with two eyes. The man has great character. Everything I always thought about him has come true and that is you can't be the best in the world unless you have something different— and that's the desire to be better than your peers. Gordon doesn't dive around like a 19-year-old goalkeeper, but he's always at the right place at the right time and makes things look so easy." As for Banks' crucial role with the Strikers, Newman said, "Gordon has given us tremendous leadership and experience at the back. Sure, he was rusty and nervous at the beginning, and we were concerned for him, but Gordon Banks has been super. The second half of the season, I saw no one better."

A crucial game against the Tampa Bay Rowdies, when both were in pursuit of the first-place Cosmos, illustrated Banks' importance. The Strikers took a two-goal lead in the first twenty minutes. First, David Proctor scored when the Rowdies poorly cleared a ball over the prone body of their goalie. Then, after a goalmouth scramble fifteen minutes later, Colin Fowles booted in the Strikers' second goal. Tampa Bay, increasingly frustrated, began taking petty fouls—tripping, holding, pushing, and the Strikers had to respond in kind. One of the Strikers' fouls resulted in a free kick that Tampa Bay's Rodney Marsh crossed to Derek Smethurst in the middle, who hit a hard, waist-high shot at Banks. The goalkeeper beat it out, but straight to the feet of Steve Wegerle, who drilled it in. After the game, Banks self-critically said, "I hit it at the wrong angle." But what he failed to mention was that few goalkeepers could have stopped the first shot.

Shortly afterward, there came a moment that recalled The Great Save of 1970. From the left, Marsh put in a beautifully hit shot that was curving just inside the right-hand post. Apparently out of the play, Banks dove full length and managed to deflect the shot. That stop and another Striker goal, by George Nanchoff, which made it 3–1 seemed to settle the contest. But the Strikers, who had played another game only two days earlier in Rochester, began showing their fatigue and the Rowdies put on more pressure. With fifteen minutes remaining, David Robb scored for Tampa Bay and suddenly the tide shifted. The Strikers' defense and Banks hung tough, however, and with the hearty support of some 10,000 hometown fans, Ft. Lauderdale preserved its one goal margin.

The game was typical of many of the low-scoring tiffs that the Strikers won during the season. Ft. Lauderdale produced a 19–7 record that made them champs of the East Division, and it was Banks who was clearly most responsible. He played every minute—that's 2,329—and gave up only 29 goals. Credited with 146 saves, he blanked opponents 9 times. Banks finished the season with a remarkable 1.12 goals-against-per-game ratio, second only to Dallas' Ken Cooper. For his work, Banks made the league all-star team in both the *Sporting News* vote (by the league's players) and the Professional Soccer Reporters Association balloting. In the *Sporting News* selection, Banks garnered 276 votes, which made him the top vote-getter.

Franz Beckenbauer placed second with 175 ballots. The PSRA, moreover, named Banks the league's Most Valuable Player.

Banks' award may have seemed pale by comparison to being named England's Footballer of the Year in 1972 or to being inducted into the Order of the British Empire (OBE) by Queen Elizabeth, but it was particularly meaningful in that all the goalkeeper was trying to do in his comeback year was get back as much of his game as possible. That Banks did, more than he thought at first was even remotely possible.

Besides his personal accomplishment, Banks was heartened by the reception soccer was getting in Fort Lauderdale and the rest of the country. He said, "Soccer is catching up quickly here. I didn't realize how well the game blended into American life and was so organized. The franchise people are taking it seriously and it is going to develop." Moreover, he believed that his play and that of his other countrymen in the NASL helped to stop some negative attitudes towards American soccer. Said Banks: "People have said that English players come here and play as if they were on holiday. We're stamping this out. The players can't take it casually for it to catch on. And we have to start with the schools first." No hollow words there, since Banks made a regular effort to visit schools and conduct clinics on the game.

For kids interested in improving their knowledge of the game in general, few players could be better to have as a teacher than Banks. For those who wanted to learn the secrets of goalkeeping, none other than Banks could speak with the same authority on the subject.

While playing with Stoke City, Banks wrote of the cardinal principles of goal tending. Said Banks: " 'Safety First'—that is the golden rule for keeping goal. Whenever you go to catch the ball, or stop it with your hands, you must always try to get part of your body behind your hands as a second barrier.

"Often when challenged, it is too risky to try to catch the

ball. It is better than to punch the ball away, preferably using both fists, towards the touchline; or to palm it behind for a corner.

"From your position on the goal-line you have the best view of what is happening in your goal area and should not hesitate to shout out clear warnings and instructions to your fellow defenders. And cover everything.

"Of course, once you have the ball in your possession, you must aim to use it constructively. Many a goal move has been started from a goalkeeper's thoughtful and accurate throw to an unmarked teammate. But as a goalkeeper, your first duty is to guard your own goal with maximum security. Never assume that a shot will go wide. Never assume anything."

This rule, said Banks, is the one "you must keep uppermost in your mind whether you are playing for a scratch team in the local park, or for England in World Cup."

Banks may have reached the pinnacle of perfection with his save in the 1970 World Cup game against Brazil, but his overall play in the 1966 World Cup competition put him on a plateau of excellence that few goalies will ever match. Banks points to the 1966 World Cup games to explain what it's like "being the last line of defense on really important occasions, the man who carried the can if anything goes wrong."

In the semifinals, England was up 2–0 against Portugal and were seven minutes away from reaching the Final when, according to Banks, "I made my first important mistake. Advancing quickly from my goal-line to try to cut off a high cross from the right, I misjudged the flight of the ball and was left stranded. Covering the goal behind me, Jack Charlton did the only thing possible to stop the ball from entering the net. He stuck out his right arm to make the save that I couldn't. His action meant that England still had a chance of a record—reaching the Finals without conceding a single goal. All I had to do to keep the slate clean was to save Eusebio's penalty shot!

"Actually a goalkeeper has little or no chance of saving

a spot kick, least of all taken by a marksman like Eusebio, the best in the whole competition. You've got to keep your feet still until the ball is hit from only 12 yards away, and as a shot from Eusebio travels at about 40 yards per second, you have only a split second in which to move."

This, Banks believes, is "the one and only situation in which a goalkeeper can forget the golden rules of 'Safety First' and 'Assume Nothing' and take a gamble. The only thing to do is make up your mind in advance which way to dive, and fling yourself that way without hesitation.

"In my time in First Division football I suppose I must have saved nearly 20 spot-kicks by diving the right way. And you needn't always guess blindly. One gets to know what to expect from the experts. Some marksmen blast the ball from the instep, relying on sheer power, but most side-foot it to the left or right of the goalkeeper, which means that you have a 50–50 chance of diving in the right direction to start with. Those are the odds which make the attempt well worthwhile."

One of Banks early attempts at guessing the direction of a penalty shot came in his first international match in April 1963 at Wembley. Said Banks: "I faced a penalty kick from Jim Baxter of Scotland with no idea of the method he might adopt. In fact, he told me afterwards that he'd never taken a penalty before. From the way he formed up I thought he would shoot to my right, so I decided to go that way. In any event, he disguised his approach run, and while I went to my right, he sent the ball flashing into the left corner of our net."

Against Eusebio, three years later, Banks thought he had a much better chance of blocking the penalty shot. "I thought I knew which way he would kick it," said Banks. "We'd all studied Eusebio's methods on TV, and discovered that in earlier matches he had invariably placed his kick to the right of the goalkeeper. That was the way I intended to go until, to my horror, as the man they call the Black Panther strolled up to place the ball, the other England lads started calling out to me and pointing to make sure I would remember our little secret. Clearly it was a secret no longer, and when I saw Cluna, the Portuguese skipper, busily briefing Eusebio, I felt sure that he was instructing the kicker to try something new, like going the other way.

" 'OK', I thought grimly. 'I'll call their bluff by diving left.' And I did. But Eusebio calmly placed the ball to the right as he always does. And as I picked it out back of the net I must have looked even gloomier of countenance than Fernandel."

With England's margin cut to one goal, the rest of the game became a matter of whether the Portuguese could convert their new hopes into a tying score. They "went flat out for the equalizer," said Banks, "and my box was a hive of industry. 'It's mine!' I cried out as a high ball sailed across from the wing, and Nobby Stiles obediently stopped in his tracks and waited for me to field it. As I went up to catch the ball, however, I accidentally struck Nobby in the back and we both went down. After getting up to play the ball down the field my first thought was for Nobby, who remained where he had fallen, rolling his head and writhing his back in apparent agony.

" 'I've really hurt Nobby,' I thought. 'He'll give me a right telling off.' Nobby got to his feet holding one hand to his ear, and the other hand to the middle of his back. Then, turning towards me, he raised both fists into the air and yelled: 'Well done, Gordon, that's it—thump me out of the way!' "

Feeling rotten about hurting Stiles, Banks soon was back in the thick of things. "In the dying minutes I made a save that helped wipe out the memory of the early embarrassment, and which gave Eusebio good reason to cry when the final whistle sounded. The brilliant Portuguese had set off on a spectacular power-run down the left flank and then, at a well-judged moment, he squared the ball to Coluna on his right. I just caught the flash of Coluna's right boot and instinctively leapt upwards and backwards to palm the ball over the crossbar for a corner. It was a near thing."

Banks added, "I really enjoyed that match against Portugal because it gave me some work to do, although after nearly 450 minutes of World Cup Football I'd been beaten for the first time. In the preceding games, England's defensive work was so sound that they scarcely needed a goalkeeper, and as any keeper will tell you, those long periods of inactivity can be dangerous because a sudden attack could catch you with concentration slipping."

England's first match, against Uruguay, which ended in a 0–0 tie, was not exactly an example of thrilling soccer. One reporter covering the match wrote that it was "like chess, except chess is much faster." Said Banks: "We knew that the Uruguayans were likely to play a defensive game and go for a draw, but we had hoped to play it swift and sure—to get a quick goal and so make them come out of their shell to open up the game where we thought we could beat them. In the event, though we created some good opportunities, our strikers couldn't finish them off. Our opponents' delight with the goalless draw was obvious—they acted as if they'd already won the Cup—whereas we were disappointed that we hadn't been able to give our supporters more to cheer about."

In England's next game, the team's confidence in being able to handle the Mexicans was well-founded and they wore down the visitors to take the match 2–0. Said Banks: "Our defense was really tight, defenders linking well with forwards and forwards coming back to help when needed. All this made my job so easy I could have got on with doing my football pools, but things happen suddenly in football and you must always be ready for a breakthrough. I remember, for example, how a deflection by an English foot took the innocence out of a long-range shot from Diaz, causing me to move a bit sharpish."

For its last qualifying round game, England took on cross-channel rival France. Two goals by Roger Hunt provided all the scoring and gave Banks' team a much easier victory than they had expected. As much as anything that occurred on the field during the game, Banks vividly re-

called a vignette that happened in the stands. Said Banks:
"Robert, my seven-year-old son was brought to see the
match, and according to my wife Ursula, proved himself
England's most patriotic supporter. When, after some thirty minutes' play without a score, Jimmy Greaves popped
the ball into the back of the French net, young Robert was
up on his feet, waving his red-white-and-blue scarf and
cheering his little head off. But the referee ruled 'offside'
and restarted the play with a free-kick against England,
whereupon Robert sat down abruptly and burst into
tears."

"'Don't worry, little boy,' said a neighboring
Frenchman, patting Robert on the arm. 'England will win,
you see, and all will be well. Vive England!'"

The quarter final match against Argentina proved to be
one of the tightest matches of the entire World Cup competition. Said Banks: "We knew this one would be hard,
and so it proved. Argentina has a strong fast-covering defense: they build up very slowly in attack but strike suddenly and effectively. In the eighteenth minute I caught a
glimpse through our massed defense of a fierce, first-time
shot from Mas and dived just in time to push the ball
around the post. Then just after we scored our goal, and
with thirteen minutes to go, Mas broke away on the left
and shot only inches wide." Banks was highly impressed
with Geoff Hurst's goal—the only one in the game and
pointed to it as offering a good lesson to all goalies—that
no matter how good you are, some shots just can't be
stopped. Said Banks: "You need to see Geoff Hurst's winning goal in slow motion to realize what a very good one it
was. The goalkeeper was well-positioned for a straightforward header into the left corner of the net, which is
where nine out of ten players would have put it. But Geoff
waited for the goalkeeper to 'assume" this, to commit
himself, then let the ball glance off his head into the other
corner; men like Hurst are a menace to goalkeepers!"

After Banks' shutout skein was broken with Eusebio's
successfully psyched penalty shot, the goalkeeper had noth-

ing else to worry about but meeting West Germany in the championship game. And that was plenty, thank you. Said Banks: "I've never been so tense as I was before the World Cup Final, even though I'd played for Leceister City in two F.A. Cup Finals at Wembley. It all seemed like a dream that I, the son of a Rotherham bookmaker, who once begged coal for living and let in twelve goals against a Sheffield works' team, should find myself part of such an historic scene."

Banks' description of the Final brings that special day at Wembley back to life: "As supporters began crowding round Hendon Hall Hotel early in the day we saw how the fervour was building up. Alf Ramsey (the England's manager) gave us the usual pre-match talk, then the coach arrived to take us to Wembley. It was only a short trip, but it seemed to take an age. I'm one who likes to get to the ground early, with plenty of time to do some loosening-up exercises and get settled.

"The atmosphere at the Stadium that afternoon was fantastic, and I knew that more than most because goalkeepers have spells of inactivity during which they can hear all that is going on—and some of it isn't all that pleasant on some grounds. However I knew that there was a job to be done to be at the best of my ability. Even if mistakes were to come—and they happen—you've just got to carry one. You can't walk off the field if you've made a mistake.

"I don't consider myself particularly superstitious, but on this occasion, as before every international match, I carried out my usual ritual of shaking each of the players by the hand and wishing him luck. One doesn't like to break a habit, especially during a winning sequence.

"Ursula was there, and I knew she'd be cheering for us though in fact she was born in Germany, where I met her while serving as a Royal Signals' dispatch rider. We were all pretty friendly with the German players, whom we'd met before, and knew that despite all that was at stake it would be a friendly and sporting match.

"After thirteen minutes play, Ray Wilson made one of

his rare slips by heading the ball to Haller's feet, and the German made no mistake with his shot. That was the second goal I let in, but Haller gave me no chance. After this England equalized, with Geoff Hurst's header from Bobby Moore's free kick, and then we went ahead in the second half with Martin Peter's goal.

"My worst moment in the entire World Cup came when Germany equalized in the last second, just when we all thought England was home and dry. The reserves had come down the lift to take part in the presentation ceremony, but Weber scored and they all had to return to their seats again while extra time was played.

"How did it happen? Well, first I remember seeing Jack Charlton go to head the ball clear from a German attacker who seemed to bend down and make a back for the tall Leeds United center-half. The ref awarded Germany a free kick which seemed scarcely justified, but no one was really worried. 'Get into line!' I yelled, and Nobby Stiles gathered our 'wall' of players round him while I took up a position which gave me the best view of the ball.

"The ball was pushed to one side for Emmerich to shoot. The latter's kick hit someone in the defensive wall, the ball ran to Held and he shot across goal. 'That's safe!' I thought. 'It'll hit the corner flag. He's missed his chance.'

"But just then Schnellinger came forward and the ball struck his arm, slowing right down in pace. It was just like a golf shot, when a player chips the ball onto the green and it suddenly falls dead. At once I saw Weber had run in and was handily placed by the far post. All arms and legs I rushed across. I could see Ray Wilson going to tackle with one foot about twelve inches above the floor so when I dived I threw myself another two feet above Ray's foot in case Weber's shot traveled higher. It did—but yet another twelve inches above my arms.

"It was a goal which made our hearts sink into our stomachs. Play was barely restarted when the final whistle sounded. Now we had to do it all over again.

"During the break before extra time Alf Ramsey came onto the field to give us fresh heart. 'You should have had this game sewn long ago,' he said. 'Now go on and show them you are the better team.'

"And that I think we did."

Indeed, the 30-minute overtime period was all England. First, Alan Ball, who had played a sparkling game during the entire match, hit Hurst with a perfectly placed pass near the left side of the West German goal. Hurst boomed a powerful shot that hit the crossbar and fell straight down. The referee ruled a goal, but Germany protested that it had not crossed the goalline. After some discussion among the officials, the goal was allowed and England led 3–2. A few minutes from the end, England got an insurance goal when Hurst scored for the third time. The hat trick was the first ever in a championship World Cup match.

The World Cup victory was a testament to Banks' immense talent. In the six games in England, the goalkeeper yielded only three tallies against the best teams in the sport. In typical Banks fashion, he offered a modest analysis of how England copped the most venerable prize in all of soccer. Said Banks: "Though I had a pretty good World Cup, England's success was strictly a team-effort and the goalkeeper in these modern times is as much a member of the team as anyone else. Complete understanding with his fellow defenders, and in particular with the center-half, is absolutely vital, and all talks and arguments we'd had in training, and on tour, to sort out 'who should do what, when' served us all in good stead. Apart from this, no one left anything to chance, everyone covered everyone else. I doubt if any international team ever had a better team spirit and understanding."

Always the perfectionist, only Banks' wrong guess about Eusebio's penalty shot could still nick the goalkeeper when recalling the World Cup of 1966. "But just for the record," he added, "we Bankses are not all mugs. My dad, a bookmaker, put his own money on England to win the World Cup when they were 20–1 outsiders!" Now, the smart money has Gordon continuing his masterful goalkeeping for the Strikers. For sure, the NASL has a winner in the man who made "the greatest save ever."

STEVE DAVID

Back in the '60s, a high school jock in Trinidad was doing 10.3 in the 100-meter dash. But the young athlete preferred another sport besides track and field. Steve David chose soccer because track involved "too much hard training. I can run all day behind a ball. But to run just like that around a track, it's tiresome."

Now, North American Soccer League goalies are finding it tiresome defending against David. With his sprinter's speed, the Los Angeles Aztec forward has become one of the most feared goal makers in the league. During the '77 season, David scored more than a goal a game, finishing with 26 tallies in 24 contests. Only an injury to his right knee, that kept him out of the season's last two games, could stop his scoring binge. Nonetheless, he walked away with the league scoring championship for the second time in three years. Put the ball on Steve David's foot near the goal, and it's like Jack Nicklaus with a five-foot putt. More often than not they'll both stroke it in.

Steve began his own putting about in Port Fortin on November 3, 1951. While young Pele kicked around a ball made of rags, Steve's earliest soccer experience came with his "running around the streets kicking oranges and grapefruits." After giving up track for soccer and finishing high school, Steve played regularly for the Trinidad national team and was named the country's Player of the Year three times. In the meantime, he had foregone his plan to join a shipping concern and, as his mother suggested, joined the island's police force. Even there, his speed afoot was an asset; more than once he was used to literally run down escaped convicts.

Spotted by American and European scouts while he played with the national team, Steve received his first professional offer in 1973 but flatly rejected it. "I really wasn't interested," he recalls, "I didn't want to play professionally. I liked police work." But the offers continued to come in—including three from NASL clubs in New York, Miami, and Dallas. Instead, Steve chose to take a two-month tryout with the Leicester City team in England.

But England presented one major problem for the Caribbean-bred player—the weather. Said Steve: "It was too cold for me so I called Miami, and said, 'OK, I'm going to come to you.' I found out that Miami was the warmest of the places I was offered a contract."

The climate suited Steve perfectly in the Sunshine State, and he provided a fresh breeze of goals for the Toros. Immediately installed in the first team, Steve scored 13 goals in 19 games and helped Miami get into the '74 championship game. The Aztecs won the title match, 4–3, on penalty shots after the teams had tied three all in regulation time. (The game was nationally televised, and the avalanche of complaints about settling the championship on penalty shots forced the league to begin considering a better way to decide winners in tied games.)

During the next season, Steve continued his high-scoring ways. Playing in 21 games, he netted 23 goals and 6 assists to win the league scoring title with 52 points. Tied for a distant second were Chicago Sting's Gordon Hill and Tampa Bay Rowdies' Derek Smethurst with 39 points. Steve also walked off with the league's Most Valuable Player Award. His only disappointment: once more the Toros bowed in the playoffs; this time in the semifinals to cross-state rival Tampa Bay by the convincing score of 3 to zip.

The '76 campaign proved to be Steve's most frustrating. The Toros management was buffeted by a hurricane of operational problems in Miami, and friction among the staff and players was a regular occurrence. For Steve, the problem was General Manager John Young. "From the time he got there, I wanted to go to another team," Steve said. The polluted atmosphere on the team ruined his game. Playing only thirteen games, the league's highest scorer the year before, got but one goal. When the Toros franchise was moved to Ft. Lauderdale, Steve was free to go with another team, and after some feelers from San Jose failed to materialize into anything solid, Los Angeles signed him.

The hope was that Steve would regain his scoring touch. Said Coach Terry Fisher: "I really felt that if we can put players in the team that can give him the kind of service he can utilize, that we'd have something special. He's proven in the league that he's a goal scorer. I think the one aspect that he has that no team can really defend is speed, sheer speed. If he can score goals, what else is there?"

Not much. And that's just what Steve did—score with amazing consistency. The season opened for the Aztecs against the Earthquakes and Steve got two goals. Next game against Hawaii, two more goals. The only worry for some was that Steve's play would suffer when English star George Best would arrive later in the spring. But Steve disagreed: "No, it's going to be great to have two good one-on-one players in Best and myself. If our teammates can't find me, they can get the ball to George and vice-versa. It's good to have the kind of player who can break a game open. Our opponents won't be able to double-team or collapse on just one of us."

Steve's confidence about not only being able to play with Best, but to be even more effective because of him, turned out to be right on. In fact, his favorite goal of the season was made with an assist from Best. Recalls Steve: "George was on the far side of the field. I got the ball from him, ran by one defender and scored. That was really something. I mean, the pass was out of this world. I never thought he could get me the ball from where he was."

Not that Steve thinks he must get perfect passes to score.

While not a boastful type, he's not shy about talking over his abilities and accomplishments. Besides his speed and his skill at taking defenders one-on-one, says Steve, "I can also put the ball where I want to. I don't have to use power or kick very hard or anything. I can place it where I want to. A goal can only be scored by a few players. When you're in the box, the pressure's really on. George can give good balls and there's nothing else you can do but score. But sometimes I've got to make the goals myself. I've got to go by maybe one or two defenders.

"I think I've got more ability than anyone in this league to score goals. I have looked at other guys and seen the chances they get and just blow. Scoring goals is a lot of pressure. You get in the box and that's where all the pressure is. That's where opponents are going to kill you, you're not supposed to be in the box.

"I think it's something I've just inherited. It's natural. I've always played up front and I've always been the leading scorer on any team I've ever played for. It's like it's built in."

Well, is there anything that is not in Steve's bag of tricks? Coach Fisher thinks so: "I think he showed in the 24 games that certainly he's not a complete player. He doesn't really play defensively, he doesn't even get behind the ball and dispossess, he hardly ever wins tackles." But Fisher is hard pressed to come up with any other criticism of his player.

In fact, the coach offers an assessment of Steve that is more laudatory than Steve's own. Says Fisher: "He might stroll around the field for 80 minutes and do nothing and in two minutes he'll score two goals. I can go through almost every game this season where that's been the case. From a coaching point of view, it's great to have a player like that that people fear because at any moment he's capable of breaking away and knocking in a goal. There are very few athletes in the world that have such breakaway speed. He's also a lot better player in the air than most people would believe. He scored a few goals with his head. He's not a physical player so he's not a typical center forward. He's certainly not a target player but he can score goals with his head and his quickness is unbelievable. I don't think there is anybody in the league who can match him for quickness."

Unfortunately for Steve, his quickness may have led to the injury that ended his '77 season. "As far as I can remember," Steve says of the incident in the game against the San Jose Earthquakes, "the ball came off [teammate's] Ron Davies' head and was hanging in the air. I was coming in and the goalkeeper [Mike Hewitt] looked like he was hesitating a bit because I looked at him first. The ball dropped right between us and I got there first. I controlled it to the inside and he came at that moment and whacked me. It was a fair tackle; he was going for the ball."

The injury to Steve's right knee ended one of the most remarkable seasons for any player in NASL history. Not only did Steve win the scoring title with 58 points (six assists as well as his 26 goals), he also set an NASL record by scoring in ten consecutive games. Moreover, he moved from seventeenth to fifth on the league's all-time scoring list. "I feel satisfied with my play this season," said Steve, "but I think I could have done better. It just gives me something to work at next year." Specifically Steve will be shooting for the NASL record of 30 goals in a season set by Chicago's John Kowalik in 1968. If anybody in the league breaks it, the sprinter-cop from Trinidad will likely be the one.

STEVE PECHER

Steve Pecher, the Dallas Tornado's superb center back, is a rarity in the NASL. He's an amateur. Entering his third year in pro soccer, Steve is paid a meager $50 a week and gets by with extra income from soccer clinics and personal appearances. Why the sacrifice? Steve is determined to play for the United States Olympic Team in 1980, as he did four years before. "There's something special about playing for your country. I really get into the national anthem."

As much as he loves to play for his country, Steve just loves the game. Raised in St. Louis with so many other American soccer standouts, he had the extra advantage of coming from a soccer family. His maternal grandfather, Gerd Kerhrman, is in the St. Louis Soccer Hall of Fame, while his older brother, Joe, was a local high school whiz who had a knack for scoring overtime goals. Steve, himself, began playing in first grade, which, he says, put him "behind the other guys—they started in kindergarten." After giving up baseball in junior high, he stuck to soccer, turning down an offer from the Normandy High football coach to kick field goals.

After he led Normandy to the state championship during his senior year, Steve enrolled at St. Louis' Florissant Valley Junior College. Steve played two years at Flo Valley, led the team to the 1975 national junior college championship, and came away from the experience with but one pro offer, and not much of one at that. It was from the St.

Louis Stars who wanted Steve to play with their farm club, the St. Louis Stripes.

Enter Flo Valley Coach Pete Sorber. At the NCAA finals that year he ran into his old friend Al Miller, coach of the Dallas Tornado, who asked Sorber if he had seen any talented youngsters around. Says Miller: "Sorber mentioned that he had an American kid, but he didn't know if he was at our level. I said, 'Well, if you recommend him, I'll fly him down to Dallas.' I thought, if nothing else, he'd be good on our reserve team."

In March of 1976, 20-year-old Steve had his first shot at the big leagues. He clearly recalls the pressure-packed trial: "When I first came here, I didn't even think about playing. I was told it was a one-week tryout, and I figured I'd be going home after a week." The first real test came in Dallas' opening preseason game against the San Jose Earthquakes. Says Steve: "I was really scared when I went in. I knew I had to prove myself. Paul Child was running me around in circles. I scored one of their goals." Miller, however, saw something that appealed to him. Just when he was about to take Steve out of the match, Child kicked him and Steve kicked him back. For the first four or five preseason games, Steve says, "I was nervous for about thirty minutes." But he got a great boost when Miller told him during that time, "You're going to make it. There's a place for you."

By the beginning of the regular season, Steve's confidence was growing, and he proved it in the home opener against the Cosmos. Assigned to mark Pele, he held the King scoreless. Even though Pele booted in a free kick to give the Cosmos a 1–0 victory, Steve was named the M.V.P. for the game and 20,000 fans at Ownby Stadium went home impressed with the Tornado's new defenseman.

Not that Steve had a lot to learn. In an early game at Seattle, he says, "we were winning 1–0 with 15 minutes left when Geoff Hurst came in. Usually I'd talk to Dick Hall [the Tornado's other center back] before the game, and he'd tell me about the players, but this time I had no preparation. Hurst ripped me to pieces and they scored two [and won]. But when we played them again in Dallas, I was ready. The second time around, I knew Hurst was strong in the air, and I played him that way." By then, Steve was getting his confidence at the beginning of the matches. "Usually if I win the first ball off my man, I think I can handle him the rest of the game."

Handling the NASL's forwards is something Steve does with special elan. At 6 feet and 195 pounds, he is big enough to play a tough game. Says Steve: "I just like the other player to know that I'm around. If he gets the ball, he'll know that someone's there to take it from him. I'm a physical player, but I'm not out there to hurt anybody, though a lot of people think I am. That's just the way I play the game. In soccer, one can express one's emotions. I'm pretty quiet off the field, but when I get on the field I'm a totally different person and I like that. When I get wrapped up in a game, sometimes I go a little too much."

Indeed, Steve's rough play has earned him the reputation around the NASL as "bad boy Peck," though he had never got a yellow warning card. It was in the World Cup qualifying games in 1976 that he received his first cards—a yellow and two reds. The first came in Vancouver, where the United States team was leading Canada 1–0 and needed the victory to go on to the next round of the World Cup elimination play. Recalls Steve: "It was in the first half and I was dribbling the ball and some guy was kicking my legs. The referee wasn't saying anything, so I kicked the other player's legs and got a yellow card.

"In the second half, there was a corner kick and a guy knocked the ball down with his arm in the penalty area. Again, the referee didn't call it. My natural reaction was to curse while running back to my position after the goalie had picked up the ball. As soon as I got to the center of the field, the referee stopped me and threw me out of the game." With only ten men for the rest of the game, the United States team could not stop Canada from scoring, and the match ended in a 1–1 tie. Steve was blamed by many Americans for the outcome.

He believes he got a bum rap. "A referee shouldn't worry about somebody cursing, he should be worrying about the fouls in the game. The thing is, this guy was a decent referee. I thought he was doing a pretty good job. I should have gotten the yellow card, but I don't think I should have been thrown out of the game."

In any event, the tie forced the two teams to play another game—in Haiti—and once again it was a closely contested affair. The Canadians were up by a goal with 18 minutes remaining; then Steve got in trouble. "I was out on the sidelines and a guy pushed the ball ahead. I went in for the ball but hit the guy instead. He did a double somersault and just lay there. The referee came over and just threw me out of the game. I thought he was going to give me a yellow card, but he threw a red on me." Undermanned for the second time, the American side gave up two more goals and was eliminated from the World Cup tourney.

While Steve's problem with refs have occurred mainly in international play, he's not too keen on the NASL's whistle-blowers either. Says he: "There are maybe two or three high-class referees in the league and from there the rest drop. The gap between the high class and the rest is too big, and the league should be doing something about it. They should have those referees train with the ones who are the best. They let me get away with things last year ['76] because it was my first year. That's what I've heard anyway. But what they really need is to have umpire teams like they have in baseball and football."

Whatever his difficulty with refs, Steve had little trouble with opponents. In his first season he tallied 111 steals, 161 defensive clearances, and 2 goals to boot. He was named the team's most valuable player in three games and was a vital element in getting the Tornado into the playoffs. His season would have been even more successful had he not suffered a shoulder separation that idled him late in the year.

Coming off the injury, Steve played one of his finest

games of the campaign. In the last game of the regular season—with Steve still out of action—the Los Angeles Aztecs pounded Dallas, 4–1. The Aztecs' Ron Davies scored two of the goals and assisted on another. Ready to play in the first round of the play-offs against Los Angeles, Steve was assigned to mark Davies, and he did such a complete job that the striker hardly touched the ball. With the Aztecs' offense shut off, Dallas counterattacked and won, 2–0.

Although the Dallas season ended poorly in the next play-off game, a 2–0 loss to the Earthquakes, Steve's exceptional work throughout the year was fully recognized. At the Soccer Bowl in Seattle, he was awarded the league's Rookie-of-the-Year silver bowl. Said Coach Miller: "Defensively, Pecher is the best American center back there is, without question."

Miller later (during the '77 season) offered a more detailed analysis of Steve's play: "He's a first-class player to work with and he wants to learn to do better. Last year, he didn't do too much in strategy, but now he has matured and is making contributions to the team in all ways. In practice, he's able to discuss problems in defense and analyze where he made mistakes and where he can improve. Last year he didn't have time to worry about that. He was just worrying about his performance."

When it comes down to Steve's performance, Miller has some criticisms but on the whole gives high ratings: "In general, his main weakness is his inexperience, which time will take care of because he's still a young boy. Specifically, his passing is weak, but I think he's working hard on that. His strength is his defending ability, his knack for reading the game, just one against one defending. Plus his competitiveness. He's an all-round player. He doesn't lack for size or strength. He has all the physical equipment and an outstanding attitude. Steve will probably become one of the top American-born players and I feel as he matures he will be an excellent leader. He has a tremendous amount of promise."

One day Steve might also become a full-fledged professional. But first there is that 1980 trip to Moscow and some *Star-Spangled Banners*, to look forward to. Says Steve: "I would really like to play in the Olympics. I want to get the United States team in there. If we could finish in the top four or five, it would really help United States soccer."

GEORGIO CHINAGLIA

"For me, America is the third step in my soccer career. I learned the game in Wales, refined it in Italy and now I want to display it in the United States." For Georgio Chinaglia, it was a typically straightforward explanation for a quite remarkable turn in his soccer career. After his school days in Cardiff, where his parents had gone from Italy to operate a restaurant, Georgio returned to Rome and established himself as the Pope's major competition for adulation. Now, on a gentle spring night in 1976, the darkly handsome, 6 ft. 1 in., 190 lb. striker was in New York, playing his first game for the Cosmos before 24,292 fans at Yankee Stadium. And Georgio did not disappoint anybody. Scoring two goals in the Cosmos' 6–0 rout of the Los Angeles Aztecs, Georgio offered immediate proof that he was all the player the team expected him to be. At 29, the man who was at the zenith of his career in Europe was on his way to a brilliant new phase of his professional life.

To appreciate the gift that North American soccer received in the coming of Chinaglia, one only has to view his record in Italy. After three seasons of Third Division play, Georgio moved to the Lazio club in Rome in 1969. For the next six years, he dominated the low-scoring Italian league's First Division and led Lazio to the national championship in 1974. Leading his team in scoring every year he was there, Georgio became both the darling and demon of the volatile soccer fans in Rome. He became accustomed to the cheers and cat-calls. "Bitterness and disillusionment," Georgio once said, "spill into the stadium on Sundays. The crowd is always looking for a scapegoat or a hero. I understand them."

And his countrymen were always aware of Georgio's dynamic presence. One Roman soccer writer summed it up: "Georgio Chinaglia has been like high-test gas in a time of great austerity. He has always been in the foreground like a star actor. In good times and bad, he has always been a leading player." It was understandable then that Italians—even those not among the thousands of Lazio's loyalists—would grieve over losing Georgio to the U.S. Said Giuseppe Chiappella, coach of Inter of Milan, "Chinaglia has been Lazio's standard bearer. He represents the life-blood of a team that has experienced wonderful moments, truly exciting, and that is now going through an absurd crisis. It's a real shame that Lazio and, above all, Italian soccer has lost such a lively talent."

Lively—and alive. One of the things about Georgio that the Italians were most upset to lose was his emotional attitude toward the game. His unexpected gesture to the coach who took him out of a World Cup game against Haiti in 1972, his visible irritation when the crowd whistled at him, his kick on the bottom for a teammate who was not playing up to par—all spontaneous acts—led sportswriters to coin the word *chinagliata* to describe Georgio's unpredictable moments. The last, as far as they were concerned, was Georgio's departure for New York. After months of speculation in the press over whether he would make the move, his actual leaving still stunned the country. How could a national hero just pick up and leave?

Georgio explained it: "I was tired of the fame in Italy and I wanted to be with my family. I met my wife, Connie, in Naples in 1969 when she was living with her father, who was stationed in the Navy there. After we got married, she moved to New Jersey, and I had to commute from Rome to the U.S. to see her. I used to come at least once a month and it got very tiring after a while. The Lazio team couldn't understand why I wanted to leave. I was the highest paid soccer player in Italy's history, but without my family it didn't mean a thing. They hated me in Italy; they called me a traitor. But it didn't bother me." When Lazio's officials tried to stop Georgio from leaving, he bluntly told them that he would simply quit the game if they did not release him. In the end, the $800,000 transfer fee the Cosmos paid Lazio did little to ease the team's or the country's bitterness.

For his new team, Georgio's arrival was greeted both with hope and trepidation. On the one hand, his scoring punch would certainly strengthen the Cosmos. On the other, there was the real question of how Georgio would be able to adjust to sharing the field—and the limelight—with the King, Pele. Gordon Bradley, then the coach, relates how it went: "I had seen Chinaglia play in Europe and he amazed me. Every time I watched him he scored a goal. I wanted to get him for the Cosmos but I didn't know how he would fit in with Pele. Chinaglia came to the Cosmos when we already had a superstar. It was Pele's new world, but it was Chinaglia's new life. But Chinaglia realized from the beginning that Pele was the star. Maybe it was because of the acceptance Chinaglia had seen Pele get when he watched a few Cosmos games in '75. There was no animosity between them. From the beginning Chinaglia gave Pele his place. That won seventy-five per cent of the battle, and he did it all himself. I never said anything to him."

From Georgio's viewpoint, nothing had to be said to him. He fully realized that Pele was Numero Uno and knew that, on talent alone, they would work well together. Said Georgio after that smashing debut at Yankee Stadium: "If you know how to play soccer, you should be able to play it anywhere in the world, and with anyone. The team realizes that when I get the ball I'm going to score or I'm going to make somebody else score. If a team stops me, Pele will score, but they can't stop both of us."

Georgio's early confidence was immediately rewarded.

In his first seven games with the Cosmos, he scored eight goals. Then he went into a slump, failing to hit the net in the next seven games. Said Georgio: "When I scored all those goals in the beginning I didn't think I had the league licked, because I knew I would hit a scoreless period. Every time I take a shot I'm thinking goal. If I don't score, it bothers me. But I knew a bad-luck streak would come." Bradley explained his new star's dilemma: "It was a delayed adjustment period. When Chinaglia first came he got all the passes and scored all the goals. But when the newness of him being on the team wore off, he didn't get the passes that he needed. I told the rest of the team to start hitting him with passes when he was on the run. He's not the kind of player who should have the ball played up to him. Chinaglia's most dangerous when he's going forward, and for a while he wasn't taking up the position where he could go forward." Indeed, unlike other center forwards who play best with their backs to the goal, almost like basketball centers, Georgio loses much of his effectiveness when he is in a "high-post" alignment.

Bradley also made another change in his fine-tuning of the Cosmos' offense. Pele who had been playing midfield was moved back up front where he and Georgio could play off each other more. The switch pleased both players. Said Pele: "What's important is that the defenders must take care of two players, not just one. Chinaglia's a very experienced player. He moves the ball very well." Added Georgio: "Bradley's move opened up more opportunities for both of us."

Georgio finally broke his slump, with a vengeance. In four games, he notched six goals. Then, to cap his re-emergence as the scoring master, as well as to finish off the regular season in style, Georgio set an NASL single-game record by scoring 12 points, on five goals and two assists, against the Miami Toros. The goals tied the league mark set by Miami's Steve David the previous year. It was an astounding performance in itself, but was made even more so by the fact that early in the game Georgio collided with

Miami goalie Van Taylor, suffered a painful shin injury and had to have three stitches in his leg during halftime. Still, after the game, Georgio was talking about another player's exploits. "I scored five," he said, "but the best goal of the night was Pele's." Georgio referred to a sensational score Pele made late in the first half when he took a pass from the right wing in the air, somersaulted, and scissor-kicked the ball past the startled Taylor. "In Brazil we call it the bicycle kick," said Pele, "and you have to be just in the right position. I have only scored about six that way in my career."

The King's spectacular shot, nevertheless, could not overshadow Georgio's flood of goals. (Even Pele had watched in awe as Georgio put in four of his goals in the last 17 minutes.) Nor could it distract Cosmo followers from the fact that Georgio had just finished a remarkable first season in America. He played every minute of the 19 games he was eligible for, led the Cosmos in shots taken with 125, a club record. In addition to the five-goal game, he had two hat tricks and three two-goal games. In all, Georgio scored 19 goals and 11 assists and captured the league's scoring title by four points over Tampa Bay's Derek Smethurst.

Though the Cosmos fell in the quarter-finals of the playoffs to Tampa Bay, 3–1, the season was a tremendous success for Georgio, as was his adjustment to America. By the end of his career in Italy, Georgio says, "Fifty million people knew my face. I had no freedom. Here I have peace." Living with his family in a $350,000 14-bedroom country house in Englewood, New Jersey, Georgio spent his off-season trying to keep in shape, setting up deals for endorsements and TV commercials, and getting to know his children better.

Keeping fit was, in a sense, a new challenge for him. Said Georgio: "I'm not used to all this time on my hands. It's a bit strange for me to have four or five months off and it takes some getting used to. Staying in shape is a major problem when you don't play for such a long time. But I am working out. In the mornings I run up and down the hills around my house. I'll run for 25 minutes without stopping, then walk for five minutes, then ten more minutes of continuous running. After that I'll do about 15 minutes of gymnastics. In the afternoons I go to a gymnasium which is close by and play some indoor soccer with friends—not an organized league or anything, just friendly games."

With his kids, Cynthia and George Jr., Georgio has a special mission. Said he: "They have forgotten they're Italian. They go to school and it's like they've been here all the time. I try to speak Italian to them at night, though. Up to a year and a half ago, they couldn't understand English and only knew Italian. Now it's the other way around. I don't want them to lose their heritage."

Georgio also worked hard trying to raise his profile in America. In his first year with the Cosmos, he was content to let center stage belong to Pele. But now that the King was retired, Georgio believed that he, among others in the NASL, should try to get more exposure. "I want to get known," he said, "not just in the New York-New Jersey area but nationwide. Soccer is a team game, but people must have idols."

Besides speaking at banquets and getting his face and name associated with sports products, Georgio got into the "Superstars" TV tournament. "I took Bob Rigby down [to Florida] as my coach," said Georgio. The former Cosmo goalkeeper had been in the competition the year before and finished fifth. "I agreed to split what I won with him. It was a good experience. I think with the way Kyle Rote was a big winner down there and Rigby finished, people are beginning to understand that soccer players are outstanding athletes. I came in fifth in my section, but I was close in everything I tried."

"I was second in the half mile and the guy who beat me was Guy Drut, the Olympic Gold Medal hurdler. I ran a 2:16. I got to the semifinals in tennis where I lost to Graig Nettles of the Yankees and he went on to win the thing, and I was fifth in the 100-yard dash, but ran a 10.8 which isn't bad. Ken Griffey of the Reds won that in something like 10.1. I had never tried to hit a baseball before I came in fifth. Some umpire taught me how to swing the bat. Keep the left elbow in and right elbow out and stop moving my head. The first time I stepped up I was really embarrassed because it seemed like such a strange sport to me. But I mastered it. Nobody likes to make a fool of himself, but the way things came out I was happy with it. Anyway, it was something to do. It's just a different world over here. I have been used to soccer and nothing else, everything centered on that one thing."

As the new season approached, Georgio said that it would be "extra important to me. It will be kind of a consecration. My number one aim is for the Cosmos to win the championship for Pele in his final season, and I want to win the scoring title again. We cannot make any mistakes because we're the team that cost all that money. People in this area won't accept rubbish. They only want the best. So when we go on the field we can't wait for a team to come to us, we have to take it to them, we have to attack. We have to win, but we also have to entertain."

When the Cosmos opened pre-season training in mid-February, Georgio was ready. Said coach Gordon Bradley: "You can tell Georgio wants to do very well this season. He's really in shape." Opposing teams in pre-season games also got Georgio's message. In the Cosmos first seven exhibition tilts, Georgio scored 8 goals. He wasn't overly impressed, however. "Even if I score 1,000 goals, that doesn't guarantee we'll draw fans. We have to win to put people in the stands. If we don't win, we can't expect to draw crowds. Normally a team needs three years to build, but here we have no time. We have to win now. And you can't fool the fans in this area. On the field I can tell. I can hear what they are saying. If you make a bad pass here you can hear the crowd rumbling, you can hear them getting restless. In Tampa you make a bad pass and they don't even know it. These fans know the game."

To buttress his point about the importance of winning in

attracting fans, he cited attendance figures. "That first season Pele came, the team drew 22,000, 24,000 and then the crowds dropped. The team wasn't winning. Last year, we drew 28,000 for our home opener, lost it and the crowds dropped. When we started winning the second half of the season the crowds picked up again."

Before Georgio could have his go at helping to pull in the crowds at Giants Stadium, the Cosmos journeyed to Europe for a couple of friendly matches. One, the game against Lazio on Rome's Olympic Stadium, was an emotional homecoming for Georgio. While a year had elapsed since the Italian team had sold him to New York, the fans had continued their protests over the move. At the game, they let team president Umberto Lenzini know that they were still angry. The crowd booed him so loudly that he was forced to leave his seat and retreat from the stadium. To make matters worse for him, Georgio scored a goal and assisted on another in the Cosmos' 2–1 victory. Said Georgio after returning to New York: "I felt sorry for Lenzini. This thing hasn't been his fault. I was the one who wanted to come to the United States. I told Lazio it was either America or I was quitting soccer." In any event, Lazio had its revenge when it came to New York later in the spring and won, 3–2. For a while, Georgio was the hero again when he scored the game's first goal midway through the first half. But Lazio tied the match one minute and 14 seconds later and went on to send the 25,803 fans who had turned out on the damp, cold night home disappointed.

More unhappy than the fans with that one game was Georgio with the season he was having. His exhibition games' output suddenly fell off at the beginning of the regular season thanks to a number of posts he hit. Over the first eight games he had only one goal and two assists. Coach Bradley observed, "He's fighting himself. As a coach all I can do is leave him to himself and encourage him when he does something well. It is something he's got to attack. He's got to play himself out of the slump and his biggest battle is with himself because he sets such a high standard to score regularly the way he has throughout his career."

While Georgio realized that there was little he could do but wait for the goals to start coming back, he thought he could benefit by some help from his teammates. Said Georgio: "I know I am having a bad season, nobody has to tell me. But I just don't fit into the style the Cosmos are playing right now. I am criticized for having my back to the goal, but I have no choice. They want me as a decoy, as a wall and I've never been that before. I cannot play with a player five yards on one side of me and one five yards on the other. This year we have so many forwards jamming in the middle there is no room, no space. I was more free in the exhibition games. I was getting the ball this way and that way. The goal area wasn't so crowded like it is now.

"I don't ever criticize another player and I don't want any player to change his style of play to accommodate me. On the field I never shout for the ball or demand it because that's not the way I was brought up in the game. But wouldn't you think that occasionally I would get some co-operation? Everybody knows that I am not good in the air, so out of 20 crosses a game would it be too much to ask for one or two of them to come low instead of high?

"I only ask two per cent. Early in the season I was getting chances and I admit I wasted them. But now I am getting three scoring chances a game and that isn't enough. They want me to challenge the goalkeeper, but I have never knocked down a goalie in my life. That isn't the way I play."

At one point during his struggle, in a game against Fort Lauderdale, Georgio dropped back into midfield and only took two shots, whereas he usually takes a dozen or so. "You won't see me doing that again," he said. "I'm there to score goals, not to be the playmaker. It's good to drop back once in a while as a change of pace, but I only did it as much as I did because I wasn't feeling completely up to par."

The crowds at Giant Stadium, expecting more from

Georgio—even though he was leading the team in scoring in late June with 8 goals and 4 assists, were quick to heckle and boo him. "I have big shoulders. I can handle it. It will come out in the end. Bad luck becomes good luck and, who knows, for all those posts I hit early in the season, maybe some impossible shots will go in just when we need them most."

Before that could happen, however, Georgio's season reached its nadir on June 27. The Cosmos played the Aztecs before an NASL record crowd of 57,192, and led by Pele's hat trick, crushed Los Angeles, 5–2. Before the game began, it was announced that Georgio would not play because of a "recurring back injury." While he did have a cold in his back that bothered one of his legs, Georgio knew full well that he was being benched for other reasons. After the game, he said, "My back's okay. I feel fine. I really couldn't see this coming."

On one hand, Georgio took the benching as a professional—"It's the coach's right to say who plays and who doesn't"—but he also could not hide his anger. He added: "In my mind this will never happen again. I'll let you finish what that means. The team won today and that's the important thing. Players may go, but the team stays."

As it happened, the coach went and the player stayed. Ten days after the benching incident, Bradley introduced Eddie Firmani, who had abruptly quit Tampa Bay, as the Cosmos new coach. The move, along with Clive Toye's mysterious resignation, suggested that Georgio was behind, or at least influenced to a greater degree than most players could, management's handling of top personnel. One player was heard to mutter the day that Bradley resigned, "Hey Georgio, who are you going to fire next?"

In fact, it wasn't all that simple. Georgio was close to Steve Ross, president of Warner Communications, the entertainment empire that owned the Cosmos, and had had his differences with both Toye and Bradley. Georgio commented on the situation: "It's no secret that I get along well with Steve Ross. I believe in the Cosmos like I believed in my old club, Lazio. Me and another man [the coach] built that club from an ordinary club to a championship team, and in two years we made $10 million. I feel the same way here. I want to play soccer, and at the same time, be a small part in making the club work. The club is professional now, and it must be run professionally, like a big business. Because that is what it is."

Asked about the resignations of Toye and Bradley, Georgio laughed: "I'm the sort of person, if I believe something should be done, I'll go all the way to see it gets done. I will put my reputation on the line for my beliefs." Ross soft-pedalled the flap: "I love Georgio, but no player, no matter who he is, can dictate who a coach is or who a president is. We listen to a lot of people and evaluate their opinions before we make those decisions."

In any event, Georgio was glad to see Toye go. "There's been ill feeling toward me from the beginning. Clive didn't want to sign me, Steve Ross wanted me. I brought Georgio Chinaglia to the Cosmos, not Clive Toye. He just got the headlines." Beyond that, the rift with Toye was fueled when he refused to renegotiate Georgio's three-year contract after he won the league scoring title. Reportedly, Georgio went to Ross and got what he wanted.

The shake-up left many of the Cosmos bewildered. Said midfielder Terry Garbett: "I just can't understand how they could let go a man like Clive Toye, who had all the contacts in the soccer world." Pele, who cried at the news of Bradley's departure, said, "I hope from now on, things will be different. I hope players now go to the coach with problems, not over his head, not behind his back."

Though the club's politics left the players wondering a bit, they knew what they had to do to get their game together. As the season wound down, there were signs that the conflict in styles was becoming less of a problem and that the team was operating more as a unit. In one of the last games, the Cosmos trounced the Washington Diplomats, 8–2, and everybody got into the act. With three goals and an assist, Georgio helped his scoring stats immensely. He finished the regular season with 15 goals and 8 assists for 38 points. That was enough to earn him fourth place in the league scoring race, pretty decent considering he called it the "worst season I've ever had."

To come, however, were the best playoffs by anyone in NASL history. In all, Georgio scored 9 goals and 19 points —both league playoff records. The biggest goal came in the championship game in Portland against the Seattle Sounders.

As expected, the Sounders came out fast. Seattle almost opened the scoring at the eight-minute mark when Jocky Scott boomed a 25-yard shot that hit a defender and caromed off the crossbar. Then a mistake by Sounder goalkeeper Tony Chursky, normally a steady netminder, gave the Cosmos a 1–0 lead. After a pass back from a defender, Chursky put the ball on the ground and was looking for a teammate upfield to clear to. Suddenly, forward Steve Hunt rushed up from behind him, poked the ball away and into the net.

The Sounders bounced back in the 23rd minute after a give-and-go play went awry at the edge of the box. The ball ended up, however, at the feet of Tommy Ord, who beat goalie Shep Messing on a low shot.

Midway through the second half, after both teams missed some excellent scoring opportunities, Nelsi Morais hit Hunt on a throw-in from the left sideline, and the game's M.V.P. raced down the flank. "There were two men on me," he said, "so the only thing I could do was put the ball across. I saw Georgio between two players and he was unmarked." The ball floated across the box and Georgio leapt to head it into the top corner, just under the crossbar. Of Georgio's 40 goals he had made for the Cosmos, it was only the third he scored with his head. Said he: "I saved it for the right time. It was the most important goal of my career. It was a beautiful pass from Stevie; I was just afraid I was going to head it over the bar. When it went in I knew we had won. It was a pretty sight."

Georgio and the rest of the Cosmos were especially

pleased to win the championship on two counts. First, of course, it was Pele's last NASL season and everybody wanted to help let him retire a champion. Secondly, after the tense season, there was nothing like a championship to heal the wounds. Said Georgio: "After all that happened this season, this victory was the greatest thing that could happen to us. Nobody thought we had a chance; they said we had a lot of problems. Well, we sorted those problems out and we're number one. That's all we have to say."

Chinaglia dribbling past Washington Diplomats defender.

Franz Beckenbauer in full stride, his eyes on the ball.

Star Cosmos Midfielder
Franz Beckenbauer.

San Jose Earthquakes Ilija Mitic moves downfield toward
the net. Maybe another goal for the leading scorer in
NASL history.

Portland Timbers Clyde Best leaps high above defender to clear the ball.

L.A. Aztecs star forward
George Best dribbling past
a defender.

George Best shows
perfect form. Notice eyes
are on the ball.

Steve David, 1977 NASL scoring champion using his speed to get past a defender.

Chicago Stings Willie Morgan moves the ball upfield.

Portland Timbers star forward Stewart Scullion heads the ball with force.

One of the all-time greats in soccer, Las Vegas Quicksilvers Eusebio.

Las Vegas Quicksilvers

Allstar Allan West of the Minnesota Kicks goes up for a header.

Minnesota Kicks

San Jose Earthquakes, Paul Child almost scores again.

ADDENDUM

ALL-TIME NASL RECORDS

INDIVIDUAL OFFENSIVE RECORDS

Most scoring points, season	69 - (30 goals, 9 assists) John Kowalik, Chicago Mustangs '68 (28 games)
Most scoring points, game	12 - Giorgio Chinaglia (New York) vs. Miami 8/10/76
Most scoring points, one-half	8 - Andy Provan (Philadelphia) vs. Washington 5/4/74 (4 goals)
Most goals, season	30 - John Kowalik (Chicago) '68 Cirilo Fernandez (San Diego) '68
Most goals, game	5 - Ron Moore (Chicago) vs. Vancouver 6/24/77; Giorgia Chinaglia (New York) vs. Miami 8/10/76; Steve David (Miami) vs. Washington 6/20/75
Most goals, one-half	4 - Giorgio Chinaglia (New York) vs. Miami 8/10/76; Andy Provan (Philadelphia) vs. Washington 5/4/74
Most consecutive games scoring a goal	10 - Steve David (Los Angeles) '77
Fastest goal	:21 - Willie Mfum (New York) vs. Rochester 8/2/71
Latest goal	90:00 - Ilija Mitic (San Jose) vs. St. Louis 5/2/75
Shortest time to score two goals	1:00 - Morrie Diane (Washington) vs. Baltimore 7/27/74; Miguel Perrichon (Toronto) vs. Montreal 8/7/73
Shortest time to score three goals	11:00 - Willie Mfum (New York) vs. Rochester 6/9/71
Shortest time to score four goals	35:00 - Andy Provan (Philadelphia) vs. Washington 5/4/74
Most goals on penalty kicks, season	8 - Keith Eddy (New York) '76

Most goals on penalty kicks, game	2 - Manfred Eickerling (Boston) vs. Rochester 7/20/74; Barry Lynch (Atlanta) vs. Lanerossi Vicenza (Italy) 6/15/71
Most penalty kicks missed, season	2 - Charlie Mitchell (Rochester) '72; Carlos Metidieri (Rochester) '71
Most assists, season	18 - George Best (Los Angeles) '77 Pele (New York) '76
Most assists, game	4 - Vito Dimitrijevic (Cosmos) vs. Toronto 6/5/77; Roberto Aguirre (Miami) vs. New York 6/14/74; Miguel Perrichon (Toronto) vs. Miami 5/6/72
Most assists, one-half	3 - Alan Wooler (Boston) vs. New York 8/3/75; Roberto Aguirre (Miami) vs. New York 6/14/74; Ian Filby (Montreal) vs. Rochester 7/17/73; Miguel Perrichon (Toronto) vs. Miami 5/6/72
Most consecutive games with an assist	5 - George Best (Los Angeles) '77; Carlos Metidieri (Rochester) '71

GOALKEEPER RECORDS

Most goals allowed, season	52 - Peter Fox (Hawaii) '77
Best goals against average, season	0.62 - Bob Rigby (Philadelphia) '73 Mirko Stojanovic (Dallas) '71
Fewest goals allowed, season	8 - Bob Rigby (Philadelphia) '73
Most shut-outs, season	12 - Lincoln Phillips (Washington) '70
Most consecutive shut-outs, season	4 - Zeljko Bilecki (Toronto) '75; Ken Cooper (Dallas) '74; Claude Campos (Rochester) '74 & '73
Most consecutive minutes without allowing a goal, one season	476 - Claude Campos (Rochester) '72
Most saves, game	22 - Mike Winter (St. Louis) vs. Rochester 5/27/73
Fewest saves, game	0 - Tony Chursky (Seattle) vs. San Jose 6/4/76; Dave Landry (Portland) vs. San Diego 6/2/76; Zeljko Bilecki (Toronto) vs. Rochester 7/6/75
Fewest saves, game, both teams	3 - Zeljko Bilecki (Toronto) 2, Jim May (Rochester) 1, 7/23/75

GOALKEEPER RECORDS *(Cont'd)*

Most saves, game, without allowing a goal	21 - Sam Nusum (Montreal) vs. Miami 5/5/73
Most minutes played, one season	2,386 - Arnie Mausser (Vancouver) '77

TEAM GENERAL RECORDS

Most games won, season	19 - Ft. Lauderdale '77; Oakland '67
Highest winning percentage, season	75% - Tampa Bay '76 (18 of 24)
Fewest games won, season	2 - Baltimore '69; Dallas '68
Lowest winning percentage, season	6% - Dallas '68 (2 of 32)
Most consecutive games won	8 - Los Angeles '74; Oakland '68
Most consecutive games without a loss (regulation time)	14 - Dallas '74
Most games lost, season	26 - Dallas '68
Most consecutive games without a victory	22 - Dallas '68
Most games tied, season (regulation time)	12 - New York '68
Highest percentage of tied games, season (regulation time)	47% - Toronto '73 (9 of 19)
Fewest games tied, season (regulation time)	1 - Baltimore '69
Lowest percentage of tied games, season (regulation time)	6% - Baltimore '69 (1 of 16)
Most tie-breakers, season	9 - Vancouver '74
Most tie-breakers won, season	6 - Miami '74
Most tie-breakers lost, season	5 - Vancouver '74; Miami '74
Most consecutive tie-breakers won, season	6 - Miami '74
Most consecutive tie-breakers, lost, season	3 - Dallas '77; Minnesota '77; Dallas '74; Boston '74; St. Louis '74

TEAM OFFENSIVE RECORDS

Most goals scored, season	71 - Oakland '68
Highest goals per game average, season	3.3 - Kansas City '69 (53 goals in 16 games)
Fewest goals scored, season	15 - Dallas '72

Lowest goals per game average, season	.88 - Dallas '68 (28 in 32 games)
Most goals, game	9 - New York (vs. Washington) 6/29/75; Oakland (vs. St. Louis) 7/26/67
Most goals, game, both teams	12 - Toronto 8, Chicago 4, 8/27/68
Largest margin of victory	9 - Oakland (9–0) vs. St. Louis 7/26/67
Most games scoring 5 or more goals, season	4 - Kansas City '68
Most games scoring 4 or more goals, season	8 - Oakland '68
Most games scoring 3 or more goals, season	14 - Oakland '68
Most games scoring 2 or more goals, season	21 - San Diego '68, Cleveland '68
Most consecutive games scoring 1 or more goals, season	24 - Minnesota '76; Chicago '68
Most goals, two consecutive games	12 - San Jose '76, New York '75
Most goals, three consecutive games	15 - Tampa Bay '76; Kansas City '68
Most goals four consecutive games	18 - Chicago '76
Most goals five consecutive games	21 - Chicago '76; Tampa Bay '76
Most goals, tie game (regulation time)	8 - Chicago at Atlanta 6/4/67; Toronto at St. Louis 8/22/67
Shortest time to score two goals, game	:15 - Ft. Lauderdale (vs. Dallas) 6/25/77
Shortest time to score three goals, game	2:00 - Philadelphia (vs. Rochester) 6/22/73; Toronto (vs. Vera Cruz-Mexico) 7/1/73
Shortest time to score four goals, game	13:31 - Seattle (vs. Hawaii) 8/4/77
Most games held scoreless	11 - Montreal '71
Fewest games held scoreless	0 - Minnesota '76; Seattle '75
Most consecutive games held scoreless	5 - Miami '76; Denver '74
Most consecutive minutes held scoreless	523 - Denver '74
Most own goals, season	4 - Dallas '77
Most shots, game	45 - Hawaii (vs. Los Angeles) 7/22/77
Most shots, game, both teams	66 - Baltimore (42) vs. San Jose (24) 5/24/76; New York (43) vs. Rochester (23) 6/9/71
Fewest shots, game	1 - Rochester (vs. Toronto) 7/6/75

TEAM OFFENSIVE RECORDS (Cont'd)

Fewest shots, game, both teams	16 - Vancouver (9) vs. Hartford (7) 5/25/75; Dallas (9) vs. Toronto (7) 5/5/73; Rochester (5) vs. Hearts-Scotland (11) 6/9/71
Most penalty kicks, game	2 - Several games
Most penalty kicks, game, both teams	3 - Dallas (2) vs. San Antonio (1) 4/18/75; Boston (2) vs. Rochester (1) 7/20/74; Dallas (2) vs. New York (1) 8/11/73; Atlanta (2) vs. Lanerossi Vincenza-Italy (1) 6/15/71
Most penalty kicks, season	8 - Cosmos '76
Most penalty kicks, missed, season	3 - Rochester '72

TEAM DEFENSIVE RECORDS

Most goals allowed, season	109 - Dallas '68
Highest average goals per game allowed, season	3.4 - Dallas (109 in 32 games)
Fewest goals allowed, season	14 - Philadelphia '73
Lowest average goals per game allowed	.74 - Philadelphia (14 in 19 games) '73
Most goals allowed, game	9 - St. Louis (vs. Oakland) 7/26/67; Washington (vs. New York) 6/29/75
Most games holding the opposition scoreless	12 - Washington '70
Most consecutive games holding opposition scoreless	4 - Toronto '75; Dallas '74; Rochester '74; Rochester '72
Most games holding opposition to one goal or none	18 - Philadelphia '73
Most consecutive games holding opposition to one goal or none	11 - Los Angeles '67
Most games holding opposition to two goals or fewer	27 - Oakland '67
Most penalty kicks against, season	8 - Toronto '71

ATTENDANCE

Largest attendance, regular season	62,394 - Cosmos (Giants Stadium) vs. Tampa Bay 6/19/77
Largest attendance, playoff game	77,691 - Cosmos (Giants Stadium) vs. Ft. Lauderdale 8/14/77
Largest attendance, international game	41,680 - Tampa Bay (Tampa Stadium) vs. Zenit-Leningrad 3/5/77
Largest total attendance, season, one club	443,847 - Cosmos (13 games) '77

Largest average attendance, season, one club	34,142	- Cosmos (13 games) '77
Largest number of sellouts, season	7	- Seattle (Memorial Stadium) '75-capacity 14,876
Largest league attendance, regular season	3,172,780	- '77 (234 games)
Largest league attendance, total	3,674,638	- '77 (251 games)
Largest average per game attendance, season	13,559	- '77 (234 games)
Largest average per game attendance, total	14,640	- '77 (251 games - includes playoffs)
Largest U.S. soccer crowd	77,691	- Cosmos (Giants Stadium) vs. Ft. Lauderdale 8/14/77

ALL-TIME PLAYOFF RECORDS

INDIVIDUAL PLAYOFF RECORDS

Most total points in playoff games, career	20 - Giorgio Chinaglia (Cosmos)
Most playoff points, one season	20 - Giorgio Chinaglia (Cosmos) 1977
Most playoff points, one game	7 - Giorgio Chinaglia (Cosmos) vs. Ft. Lauderdale 8/14/77 (3 goals, 1 assist)
Most goals in playoff, career	9 - Giorgio Chinaglia (Cosmos)
Fastest goal in playoffs	1:30 - Joe Jelinek (Boston Minutemen) vs. Baltimore Bays, 1974
Latest goal in playoffs	176:00 - Carlos Metidieri (Rochester Lancers) vs. Dallas Tornado 9/1/71
Shortest time to score two goals	:47 - Des Backos and Charlie Cooke (Los Angeles Aztecs) vs. Dallas 8/17/77
Shortest time to score three goals	3:29 - Miro Rys, Des Backos, Charlie Cooks (Los Angeles Aztecs) vs. Dallas 8/17/77
Most playoff assists, one season	7 - Steve Hunt (Cosmos) '77
Most playoff assists, career	7 - Steve Hunt (Cosmos)
Most assists, one game	3 - Steve Hunt (Cosmos) vs. Tampa Bay 8/10/77

GOALKEEPERS RECORDS

Most goals allowed in playoffs, career	18 - Ken Cooper (Dallas)
Best goals against average, one season	0:00 - Paul Hammond (Tampa Bay) 1975 (3 games); Bob Rigby (Philadelphia) 1973 (2 games)
Best goals against average, career	(need 270-0.69 minutes) Zeljko Bilecki (Toronto) (5 goals, 652 minutes)

Fewest goals allowed one season	0 - Bob Rigby (Philadelphia) 1973; Paul Hammond (Tampa Bay) 1975
Most shutouts, career	3 - Paul Hammond (Tampa Bay); Ken Cooper (Dallas); Zeljko Bilecki (Toronto); Jack Brand (Rochester)
Most saves, one game	17 - Mirko Stojanovic (Dallas) vs. Rochester, 9/14/71; Jerry Sularz (Cosmos) vs. Dallas, 8/15/73
Fewest saves, one game	1 - Jack Brand (Rochester) vs. Toronto 8/13/77; Jack Brand (Rochester) vs. Cosmos 8/22/77
Most goals allowed, one season	10 - Gordon Banks (Ft. Lauderdale) 1977

TEAM RECORDS

Most playoff games won	9 - Cosmos (2 in '72, 1 in '76, 6 in '77)
Best winning percentage	1.000 - Philadelphia (two wins in two games)
Lowest winning percentage	0.000 - Vancouver (0 wins in two games)
Most consecutive games won	6 - Cosmos 1977
Most playoff games participated in	15 - Dallas

TEAM OFFENSIVE RECORDS

Most playoff goals, career	28 - Cosmos
Highest average goals per game, career	2.25 - Miami/Ft. Lauderdale (9 goals in 4 games)
Most goals, one game	8 - Cosmos (vs. Ft. Lauderdale) 8/14/77
Most goals, two teams, one game	8 - Cosmos 3 - Ft. Lauderdale 8/14/77 at Giants Stadium
Most games scoring one or more goals	12 - Dallas
Most penalty shot goals	1 - Joe Jelinek (Cosmos) vs. St. Louis, 8/26/72; Jim Fryatt (Philadelphia) vs. Toronto, 8/18/73; Tommy Ord (Seattle) vs. Minnesota, 8/17/77
Most shots, one game	38 - Portland (vs. Seattle) 8/12/75
Fewest shots, one game	6 - San Jose (vs. Minnesota) 8/28/76
Fewest shots, two teams	21 - Minnesota (15) vs. San Jose (6) 8/25/76
Most shots, two teams	55 - Cosmos (31) at Ft. Lauderdale (24) 8/17/77 Cosmos (29) vs. Seattle (26) 8/28/77

TEAM OFFENSIVE RECORDS (Cont'd)

Most games held scoreless	4 - Toronto
Fewest games held scoreless	0 - Philadelphia (2 games)

TEAM DEFENSIVE RECORDS

Most goals allowed, career	23 - Dallas
Fewest goals allowed, one season	0 - Tampa Bay (3 games) 1975
Most games held opposition scoreless	4 - Dallas, Seattle
Most games held opposition to one goal or less	9 - Cosmos
Most goals allowed, one season	11 - Ft. Lauderdale (2 games) 1977

ATTENDANCE RECORDS

Largest playoff attendance	77,691 - Cosmos (Giants Stadium) vs. Ft. Lauderdale 8/14/77
Largest playoff total attendance, one season	501,858 - 1977 (17 games)
Largest playoff average attendance	29,521 - 1977 (17 games)
Largest team total attendance, one season	212,410 - Cosmos 1977 (3 games)
Largest average per game attendance, one team, one season	70,803 - Cosmos 1977

NASL HONOR ROLL

NASL MOST VALUABLE PLAYER

1967 – Ruben Navarro (Philadelphia Spartans)
1968 – John Kowalik (Chicago Mustangs)
1969 – Cirillio Fernandez (Kansas City Spurs)
1970 – Carlos Metidieri (Rochester Lancers)
1971 – Carlos Metidieri (Rochester Lancers)
1972 – Randy Horton (New York Cosmos)
1973 – Warren Archibald (Miami Toros)
1974 – Peter Silvester (Baltimore Comets)
1975 – Steven David (Miami Toros)
1976 – Pele (New York Cosmos)
1977 – Franz Beckenbauer (New York Cosmos)

NASL ROOKIE OF THE YEAR

1967 – Willie Roy (Chicago Spurs)
1968 – Kaizer Motaung (Atlanta Chiefs)
1969 – Siegfried Stritzl (Baltimore Bays)
1970 – Jim Leeker (St. Louis Stars)
1971 – Randy Horton (New Orleans)
1972 – Mike Winter (St. Louis Stars)
1973 – Kyle Rote, Jr. (Dallas Tornado)
1974 – Douglas McMillan (Los Angeles)
1975 – Chris Bahr (Philadelphia Atoms)
1976 – Steve Pecher (Dallas Tornado)
1977 – Jimmy McAlister (Seattle Sounders)

NASL CHAMPIONS

1967 – Oakland Clippers (NPSL)
1967 – Los Angeles Wolves (USA)
1968 – Atlanta Chiefs
1969 – Kansas City Spurs
1970 – Rochester Lancers
1971 – Dallas Tornado
1972 – New York Cosmos
1973 – Philadelphia Atoms
1974 – Los Angeles Aztecs
1975 – Tampa Bay Rowdies
1976 – Toronto Metros
1977 – New York Cosmos

NASL RUNNERS-UP

1967 – Baltimore Bays
1967 – Washington Whips
1968 – San Diego Toros
1969 – Atlanta Chiefs
1970 – Washington Darts
1971 – Atlanta Chiefs
1972 – St. Louis Stars
1973 – Dallas Tornado
1974 – Miami Toros
1975 – Portland Timbers
1976 – Minnesota Kicks
1977 – Seattle Sounders

NASL LEADING SCORER

Year	Player–Team	Games	Goals	Asts.	Points
1967	Yanko Daucik (Toronto Falcons)	17	20	8	48

Year	Player–Team	Games	Goals	Asts.	Points
1968	John Kowalik (Chicago Mustangs)	28	30	9	69
1969	Kaiser Motaung (Atlanta Chiefs)	15	16	4	36
1970	Kirk Apostolidis (Dallas Tornado)	19	16	3	35
	Carlos Metidieri (Rochester Lancers)	22	14	7	35
1971	Carlos Metidieri (Rochester Lancers)	24	19	8	46
1972	Randy Horton (New York Cosmos)	13	9	4	22
1973	Kyle Rote, Jr. (Dallas Tornado)	18	10	10	30
1974	Paul Child (San Jose Earthquakes)	20	15	6	36
1975	Steven David (Miami Toros)	21	23	6	52
1976	Giorgio Chinaglia (New York Cosmos)	19	19	11	49
1977	Steve David (L.A. Aztecs)	24	26	6	58

NASL LEADING GOALKEEPER

Year	Player–Team	Games	Saves	Goals	Shut-outs	Aver.
1967	Mirko Stojanovic (Oakland Clippers)	29	NA	29	10	1.00
1968	Ataulfo Sanchez (San Diego Toros)	22	130	19	NA	0.93
1969	Manfred Kammerer (Atlanta Chiefs)	14	56	15	4	1.07
1970	Lincoln Phillips (Washington Darts)	22	96	21	12	0.95

Year	Player–Team	Minutes	Saves	Goals	Shut-outs	Aver.
1971	Mirko Stojanovic (Dallas Tornado)	1359.00	91	11	8	0.79
1972	Ken Cooper (Dallas Tornado)	1260.00	107	12	6	0.86
1973	Bob Rigby (Philadelphia –Atoms)	1157.00	78	8	6	0.62
1974	Barry Watling (Seattle Sounders)	1800.00	132	16	8	0.80
1975	Shep Messing (Boston Minutemen)	1639.32	140	17	6	0.93
1976	Tony Chursky (Seattle Sounders)	1981.00	135	20	9	0.91
1977	Ken Cooper (Dallas Tornado)	2100.00	120	21	8	

GLOSSARY OF SOCCER TERMS

CENTER - to pass the ball from a wide position on the field into the penalty area.

CHARGE - pushing the opponent off balance legally by shoulder-to-shoulder contact.

CLEAR - a throw or kick by the goalkeeper, or a kick by the defender in an attempt to get the ball away from the goal area.

CROSS - same type of pass as center.

DEFENDER - primarily a defensive player who assists the goalkeeper in protecting the goal.

DRIBBLE - a way of advancing the ball past defenders by a series of short kicks with one or both feet.

FORWARD - primarily an attacking player whose responsibility is to create and score goals.

GOALKEEPER- the last line of defense. The only player who can use his hands within the field of play. He is limited to using hands only within the penalty area.

HALF-
VOLLEY - kicking the ball just as it is rebounding off the ground.

HANDS - illegal act of intentionally touching the ball with the hands or arms.

HEADING -   a method of scoring, passing, and con-
              trolling the ball with the head—
              without the use of hands or arms.

LINKMAN -   another name for midfielder.

LOB -   a high, soft kick taken on the volley,
              lifting the ball over the heads of the op-
              ponents.

MARKING -   guarding an opponent.

MID-
FIELDER -   is both an offensive and defensive
              player who is primarily responsible for
              linking the forwards and defenders.

OBSTRUCTING -
              preventing the opponent from going
              around a player by standing in his
              path.

OVERLAP -   the attacking play of a defender going
              down the touchline past his own
              winger.

PITCH -   another name for the field of play.

SAVE -   the goalkeeper stopping an attempted
              goal by catching or deflecting the ball
              away from the goal.

SCREEN -   retaining possession and protecting the
              ball by keeping the body between the
              ball and opponent.

SLIDING
TACKLE -   attempting to take the ball away from
              the opponent by sliding on the ground.

STRIKER -   a central forward position in the team
              with a major responsibility for scoring
              goals.

SWEEPER -   a defender who roams either in front
              of, or behind, the defender line to pick
              up stray passes.

TACKLING -   attempting or taking the ball away
              from an opponent when both players
              are playing the ball with their feet.

TRAP -   controlling a ball passed close to the player by means of the feet, thighs, or chest.

VOLLEY -   kicking the ball while it is in flight.

WALL PASS - a pass to a teammate followed by a first-time return pass on the other side of the opponent (give-and-go).

WING -   an area of the field near the touchline.

WINGER -   name given to the right and left outside forwards.

4-3-3 -   the player formation most used today (a goalkeeper, four defenders, three midfielders, and three forwards).

4-2-4 -   most used alternation formation to the 4-3-3 (a goalkeeper, four defenders, two midfielders and four forwards).

CONDENSED RULES OF SOCCER

RULE 1 - *The Ball* (NASL approved ball - Adidas) circumference 27"–28", weight 14 oz. – 16 oz.

RULE 2 - *Number of players.* Each team consists of 11 players, one of whom must be the goalkeeper. A maximum of three substitutes may be used.

RULE 3 - *Player equipment.* Consists of a shirt, shorts, stockings, and shoes. Goalkeeper must wear colors which distinguish him from the other players.

RULE 4 - *Referees.* One referee is appointed for each match. He is responsible for control of the game and his decisions are final.

RULE 5 - *Linesmen.* Two linesmen assist the referee by indicating offside, when the ball is out of play, and which team is entitled to the corner kick or throw in.

RULE 6 - *Duration of the game.* Shall be two equal periods of 45 minutes unless otherwise agreed upon.

RULE 7 - *The start of play.* A flip of a coin decides which team will kickoff. Each team must stay on its own half of the field, and the defending players must be at least 10 yards from the ball until it is kicked.

After a goal, the team scored upon will kickoff.

After halftime, the teams change ends and the kickoff will be taken by the opposite team to that which started the game. A goal cannot be scored directly from a kickoff.

RULE 8 - *Ball In and Out of Play.* The ball is out of play when (a) it has wholly crossed the goalline or touchline, whether on the ground or in the air, or (b) when the game has been stopped by the referee.

RULE 9 - *Method of Scoring.* A goal is scored when the whole of the ball has passed over the goalline, between the goalposts and under the crossbar.

RULE 10 - *Offside.* A player is offside if he is nearer his opponents' goalline than the ball at the moment the ball is played unless (a) he is in his own half of the field of play (b) there are two of his opponents nearer to their own goalline than he is (c) the ball last touched an opponent or was last played by him or (d) he receives the ball direct from a goal kick, a corner kick, a throw in, or when it was dropped by the referee. *Note:* This is the Traditional Rule. In 1973 NASL introduced a "Blue Line" Concept with a line drawn the width of the field 30 yards from each goal. Under it, an attacking player is not offside until he is within 35 yards of his opponents' goal rather than midfield, as under the Traditional Rule.

RULE 11 - *Fouls and Misconduct.* A player who intentionally attempts to, or actually; (1) kicks, (2) trips, (3) jumps at, (4) charges violently, (5) charges from behind, (6) strikes, (7) holds, (8) pushes an opponent, or (9) intentionally handles the ball shall be penalized by a direct free kick. Any one of these nine offenses committed in the penalty area by a defender will result in a penalty kick to the offensive team. A player committing less flagrant violations such as offside, dangerous plays, obstruction, or ungentlemanly conduct will be penalized by an indirect free kick.

RULE 12 - *Free Kicks*. Are classified into two categories: "Direct" (from which a goal can be scored directly against the offending side), and "Indirect" (from which a goal cannot be scored unless the ball has been touched by a player other than the kicker before entering the goal). For all free kicks, the offending team must be at least 10 yards from the ball until it is kicked.

RULE 13 - *Penalty Kick*. A direct free kick taken at the penalty mark. All players, except the player taking the kick and the goalkeeper, must stay outside the penalty area and at least 10 yards from the ball (hence the arc at edge of penalty area).

RULE 14 - *Throw In*. When the ball has wholly crossed the touchline, it is put back into play by a throw in from the spot where it went out and by a player from the opposite team that last touched it. A goal cannot be scored directly from a throw in.

RULE 15 - *Goal Kick*. When the ball has wholly crossed the goalline after being last touched by a player from the attacking team, it is put back into play by a kick from the goal area by the defending team.

RULE 16 - *Corner Kick*. When the ball has wholly crossed the goalline after being last touched by a player from the defending team, it is put back into play by a kick from the corner, on the side the ball went out by the attacking team.

THE TIE BREAKER RULE—THE SHOOTOUT

NASL games which are tied at the end of regulation play will be extended by 15 minutes of "sudden death" overtime (two 7½ minute periods). A flip of the coin will decide which team will kick off. The first team to score a goal, either from the field or by penalty kick, shall be the winner. If no score occurs in the first period, play shall be halted by the referee. The teams will change ends of the field. Play will be restarted with a kickoff by the team opposite that which started the overtime period.

If the game remains tied at the end of the second overtime period, the outcome will be decided by The Shootout which involves players on each team challenging the opposing goalkeeper in a one-on-one situation.

The visiting team will kick first and each team will take five chances in alternate order. Attacking players will start with the ball on the 35-yard line and must take their shot within five seconds. Goalkeepers have no movement restrictions within the five-second period.

The kicks shall be ended when one team has achieved an insurmountable advantage, such as scoring on its first three kicks, and their opponents miss their first three.

If the teams remain tied after the prescribed five attempts, they shall continue to take alternate kicks until one has scored more than the other after an equal number of attempts. Only players left in the game at the end of the overtime period shall be eligible to take such kicks. No player may take a second kick until all other eligible members of his team have done so, at which time they shall continue in any order the team may wish, i.e. they do not have to kick in the same rotation.